TAKING THE AMERICAS FOR JESUS

TAKING THE AMERICAS FOR JESUS

BY JOSHUA SCHWISOW
EDITED BY R.A. SHEATS

Printed in the United States of America
1st Printing, 2021

ISBN: 978-1-954745-13-1

Chapter 23 written by R.A. Sheats.

Cover Design: Justin Turley
Interior Layout Design: Sarah Lee Bryant

Published by:
Generations
19039 Plaza Drive Ste 210
Parker, Colorado 80134
www.generations.org

For more information on this and
other titles from Generations,
visit www.generations.org or call 888-389-9080.

CONTENTS

CONTENTS

INTRODUCTION FOR PARENTS AND TEACHERS

Dear Parents and Teachers,

Thank you for choosing *Taking the Americas for Jesus* for your student's history studies. Before your student gets started, here is some introductory information so that you can make the best use of this course.

Taking the Americas for Jesus contains twenty-six chapters retelling some of the most significant stories from Christian history in the Americas. Because this course is designed for third grade readers, it is necessarily limited in its scope. We've selected some of our favorite stories, but many stories that could be told were not included. We hope this book will whet your appetite and your student's appetite for further studies in this area. History has laid up for us many more wonderful works of God on the American continents. You will find that later courses produced by Generations contain many of those stories.

Many of the chapters in this book are biographical in nature. We use biography to teach history for a few reasons. First, this biographical approach immerses the reader into a particular place and time with living color. The student gets to "see the sights" and "hear the sounds" by reading stories of real people. We also use biography because God accomplishes His purposes through faithful messengers. The gospel of Jesus Christ is spread throughout the world by His servants.

WHY THE TITLE?

In 2017, Generations published a high school textbook called *Taking the World for Jesus*. Within that book, author Kevin Swanson recorded the history of the spread of Christ's church from Jerusalem in the first century to the ends of the earth. To be used alongside this work, we have prepared books that retell this history continent by continent for younger children by focusing on a single area of the world and delving into greater detail in the stories contained in each volume. These stories chronicle Jesus Christ's rule as it is recognized and acknowledged throughout the world. Scripture tells us that He is Ruler over all kings on earth (Rev. 1:5). The stories in this series of history books recount in a small way how Jesus' rule was both further established and recognized all over the world.

The title *Taking the Americas* is not intended to be a reference to colonialism. Of course, we are grateful that the Christian faith was spread around the world through European colonial efforts. But not every aspect of colonialism was righteous. Nor was every colonial effort a Christian effort. This book focuses on how the Christian message reached the Americas, not on how Spain or Britain took the Americas.

A LOOK AT THE CHAPTERS

The textbook begins with two introductory chapters focused on geography. In these chapters, the student will learn about North, South, and Central America. This material is intended to orient the reader to the locations and sights they will encounter in the stories that follow. The third chapter briefly explores the question, "How did native Americans get to the Americas?" It details some of the archaeological remains that inform us about the civilizations located in the Americas before the arrival of Europeans. Chapters 4-6 retell the stories of the first European explorers including Leif Erickson, Christopher Columbus, and the Spanish Conquistadors.

The remaining chapters bounce back and forth between stories covering North America and South America. You will find some of the most familiar stories of American history such as the *Mayflower* Pilgrims, David Brainerd, and George Whitefield. But we've also tried to include some lesser-known figures such as Jens Haven, the Dane who took the gospel to the Eskimos of Labrador, W. B. Grubb, the missionary to Paraguay, the Indian Clah who shared the gospel with his own people in Alaska, and more.

In our retelling of the historical accounts, we have striven for historical accuracy. To engage the young reader, we have introduced dialogue into the stories. Some of this dialogue is taken directly from primary sources but simplified for younger readers. In some cases, fictional dialogue is supplied. These dialogue portions portray "what might have been said" based on what we know about the events.

In this book, the terms *native*, *native American*, and *Indian* are generally used interchangeably. We understand that *Indian* is not historically accurate as Columbus never did discover the *Indies*. But, since the time of Columbus' original error, the term *Indian* has stuck and is often used in historical writings past and present. The historical circumstances of how *Indian* became a designation for native Americans is explained to the student in the chapter on Christopher Columbus.

In order to make this course visually engaging, we have provided maps, historical artwork and photography, and some custom illustrations. Taking time to examine the maps will help the student gain a grasp of the geography of the area they are studying.

This course also contains Prayer Points. These are suggested topics to guide the reader into a time of prayer. We should give thanks and praise to God for His great works done in the past. And we should pray that God's kingdom would come and His will be done in the future. It is recommended that the parent/teacher and student take time to pray together after each chapter is read.

In a few places, we have used a paraphrase of Scripture (taken from the New International Reader's Version) in order to communicate the meaning of some passages in a more simple way for young readers. The use of the NIrV should be seen as an interpretive rendering of the verses. Parents may consult a more formal translation such as the New King James Version if they wish.

A workbook to accompany *Taking the Americas for Jesus* is also available. It contains a lesson schedule, written assignments, and enrichment projects to further reinforce the material introduced in this book.

We offer this resource to Christian families around the world with the prayer that Jesus Christ, our Great King and Savior, would be glorified in its use and in our humble efforts to record His marvelous works in history.

For Christ's Kingdom,
Joshua Schwisow
January 2021

Buffalo in Grand Teton National Park, Wyoming

NORTH AMERICA

1

O Lord, our Lord,
How excellent is Your name in all the earth! (Psalm 8:9)

Welcome to the Americas! In this book, you will learn about what God has done in this part of the world. In the last 2,000 years, much has changed in the Americas. This book tells just a few stories about this change. It is an exciting story. It is exciting because God is the Lord of history. God is wise. God is good. God has a plan.

Two thousand years ago, the Lord Jesus rose from the dead. He then went to heaven. In heaven, Jesus rules over the world. The Bible says that Jesus is King over all things (Rev. 1:5). He has all power (Matt. 28:18-20). This means that He is ruling over the Americas. One day, every person on earth will bow to Jesus. They will confess that He is Lord.

Right now, the good news of the gospel is spreading. God is saving people everywhere. All over the world, people are learning that Jesus rules and reigns.

Long ago, people in the Americas believed in false gods. But now, many people here follow Jesus. How did this happen? Why did these people change? In the past, men and women came to America. These men and women loved and served God. They told the people in this land about the good news. Many of these people learned to believe in God and worship Him.

Soon you will read stories about these people. But first, we'll learn a little about **geography**. Geography is a big word. It teaches us what a land is like. It tells us about the mountains, rivers, forests, and other things in a land. It tells us if a land is hot or cold or wet or dry.

The land of America is split into two **continents**. A continent is a large piece of land bordered by ocean. North America is one continent. South America is the other. In this chapter, we will learn about North America.

MAJOR COUNTRIES IN NORTH AMERICA

North America has three large countries in it. They are the United States of America, Canada, and Mexico. Canada is in the north. Mexico is in the south. And the United States is in the middle.

The United States has the most people in it. About 330 million people live here. This country has fifty states in it. Forty-eight of these states are joined to each other. But two of the states don't touch the rest. These two states are far away from the others. Their names are Alaska and Hawaii. Alaska is beside Canada. Hawaii sits all by itself in the middle of the ocean. Most people in the United States speak English.

Canada is larger than the United States. But not as many people live here. Most of the people live near the border. This border divides the United States from Canada. Not many people live in the north parts of Canada. It's hard to live in the north because it gets so cold up there. Canada is filled with mountains, rivers, trees, and animals. It is a beautiful land. It the second largest country in the world. Only Russia is bigger than it is. People in Canada speak English and French.

Far to the south is Mexico. Because it is so far south, Mexico has much warmer weather. It also has more people than Canada. In Mexico you can find some of the oldest buildings in the world. Long ago, the Aztecs and Mayans built large cities here. You will learn more about these nations in later chapters. People in Mexico speak Spanish.

MAJOR COUNTRIES IN NORTH AMERICA

Country	Population
United States of America	330 million
Mexico	131 million
Canada	38 million

Big Sur Bridge, California

Banff National Park, Alberta, Canada

MOUNTAINS

Before the mountains were brought forth,
Or ever You had formed the earth and the world,
Even from everlasting to everlasting, You are God. (Psalm 90:2)

Every part of God's creation shows us His glory. We see God's wisdom, power, and beauty by looking at the earth. What do you think of when you look at a mountain? You might think about how strong God must be to make such a big, tall thing. North America has many **mountain ranges**. A mountain range is a group of mountains in a long line.

The tallest mountain in North America is in Alaska. It is called Mt. Denali. This mountain is 20,310 feet tall. Because it is in Alaska and because it is very tall, it can get very cold on top of the mountain. If you ever climb to the top, you will need a lot more than just a coat! Sometimes it gets as cold as 100° below zero. Even during the summer, the top of the mountain will be freezing cold.

Mt. Denali, Alaska
Pico de Orizaba

If we go down to Mexico, we will find another tall mountain. This one is called Pico de Orizaba. It is the tallest mountain in Mexico. It is 18,491 feet tall. Because this mountain is so far south, it is not as cold as Mt. Denali. But there is always snow at the top of this mountain. Even in summer, the snow never melts.

HIGHEST MOUNTAINS IN NORTH AMERICA		
Mountain	**Elevation**	**Location**
Mt. Denali	20,310 feet	Alaska, USA
Mt. Logan	19,551 fee	Yukon, Canada
Pico de Orizaba	18,491 feet	Veracruz, Mexico

Mississippi River

Yukon River

RIVERS

The earth is the LORD's, and all its fullness,
The world and those who dwell therein.
For He has founded it upon the seas,
And established it upon the waters.
(Psalm 24:1-2)

Without water, we could never survive. We need water to stay alive. People use water to drink, to cook, and to clean. They also use it to water their crops. Because the Lord is full of grace, He gave America many rivers and lakes. This is a sign of His mercy to the people here. Many cities are built near rivers. People built cities near rivers because the water helps them survive.

One of the largest rivers in North America is the Mississippi River. Take a break from reading here. Try to spell Mississippi. Can you do it?

The Mississippi is over 2,000 miles long. Look at the map to find some big cities that were built beside this river. It is a very wide and long river. Because it is so long, it is very useful. For hundreds of years, people have used this river for moving food and supplies from one place to another.

Another very long river is the Yukon. It flows through Canada. The waters of the Yukon flow all the way into the ocean. This river helps many people by bringing them lots of fish. The Yukon abounds with salmon. Because this river is so far north, it can get very cold. There are many small towns along the river. In one of the towns, it might get as cold as 28° below zero. That's very cold! There are no roads to many of these little towns. People use the Yukon River as a water road to bring in food and other things they need.

Much further south, there is the mighty Rio Grande River. How do you think this river got its name? The name is Spanish, and it means "Big River." Just like its name says, it is a very big river. It divides Texas from Mexico.

MAJOR RIVERS IN NORTH AMERICA		
River	**Length**	**Location**
Missouri River	2,341 miles	USA
Mississippi River	2,320 miles	USA
Yukon River	1,980 miles	Alaska, Canada
Rio Grande	1,896 miles	USA, Mexico

Grand Canyon, Arizona

BEAUTIFUL PLACES IN NORTH AMERICA

O Lord, how manifold are Your works!
In wisdom You have made them all. (Psalm 104:24)

God's beauty and glory is found all over His creation. North America has many beautiful places. Perhaps you can visit some of them.

Are you looking for a lovely sunrise? You might see one if you ever go to Arizona. This is where you will find the Grand Canyon. The Grand Canyon is so big and so amazing that you might gasp when you see it. We call it a breathtaking sight. This is one of the most amazing places in the world. The Canyon is about 270 miles long. At points, it is eighteen miles wide. In this canyon, you will see many kinds of rock layers.

Would you like to see some polar bears? Take a trip to the town of Churchill. This town is in the far north of Canada. Yes, it is hard to get there. And you will need a very warm jacket. But in Churchill, you can see polar bears up close. This town is called the "Polar Bear Capital of the World."

If Churchill is too cold for a visit, you could go south. Take an airplane down to Mexico. Instead of snow and ice, you will find tropical jungles. Instead of polar bears, you will find lots and lots of bugs. Here, in a place called Yucatan, you will find something very strange. This part of Mexico has a number of **cenotes** (pronounced "suh-no-tees"). These are underground lakes or ponds. The sun shines through a hole in the ceiling onto the water below. There are over 6,000 cenotes in Yucatan.

Polar bears in Churchill, Manitoba, Canada

Another thrilling sight is found on the border of Canada and the US. There you will find Niagara Falls. Niagara Falls has three large waterfalls. Water drops over 150 feet into the river below. If you get too close to the falls, you won't be able to hear anything. The water is too loud! The falling water makes a sound louder than thunder.

Now you've seen a little of the vast continent of North America. What should we do after seeing all these wonderful things? We should stop and praise God. This land shows us His great power and majesty. Can you see His power in these mighty mountains? Can you see His majesty in the beauty of His creation?

PRAYER POINTS: NORTH AMERICA

Take time now to pray a prayer of praise. Let us adore and worship our great God!

- **Praise God for His Power**
  We learn much about God by studying creation. We learn how powerful our God is when we see Niagara Falls. The Lord by His power made Mt. Denali to stand. The God who made all things is worthy of our praise.

- **Praise God for His Goodness**
  We live in a fallen world. All the world is wounded by the fall into sin. But God is still good to His creation. He continues to send us sunshine to give us warmth. He sends rain to the peoples of North America so they can eat. He gives them rivers for food and travel. Behold the goodness of God. Praise Him for this goodness!

Niagara Falls

Vinicunca, Cusco Region, Peru (called in English, “Rainbow Mountain”)

SOUTH AMERICA AND CENTRAL AMERICA

2

He sends the springs into the valleys;
They flow among the hills. . . .
He waters the hills from His upper chambers;
The earth is satisfied with the fruit of Your works.
(Psalm 104:10, 13)

You took a brief tour of North America. Now let's go south. Next up is South America and Central America. South America is a little smaller than North America. But it is still a giant! It is the fourth largest continent in the world.

Because it's so big, you can find many kinds of land here. You'll find snowy mountains and deserts. You'll see rivers and rainforests. Tall trees, flat plains, and more are all a part of this vast land.

In every place you look, you'll find God's beauty. Our God is powerful. He is also a wise Creator. He created many kinds of land, and each kind has its own special weather. He forms tall mountains. He stretches out the rivers. In some places, He pours down abundant rain. In others, He makes the weather very dry.

Look at the northern part of South America. This area is tropical. That means it has warm weather all year long. Here you'll find warm beaches and tall palm trees. You'll also see many beautiful animals.

Now look at the southern part. It gets much colder there. Why is the southern part of South America colder? It's because the southern tip of this land is only 600 miles from Antarctica. Because of this, many types of penguins live here.

CARACAS, VENEZUELA

Caracas, the capital of Venezuela, is a tropical city. The weather here stays warm all year long, in summer and winter.

As you can see, there are many kinds of places in South America. Perhaps you can visit them someday.

South America and Central America

MAJOR COUNTRIES IN SOUTH AMERICA

Next, let's look at a few of the largest nations in South America. We don't have time to learn about every country right now. But in later chapters of this book, you will discover much more about them.

The biggest nation on this continent is Brazil. This is the largest nation by land size. It also has the most people in it. Most of the people in Brazil live near the ocean. But Brazil also has much land that is far from the coast. This land is covered in mountains and jungles. Deep within Brazil, you will find the marvelous Amazon Rainforest.

Far to the north of Brazil, you will find the nation of Colombia. It is much smaller than Brazil, but more than fifty million people live there. Colombia has a long coastline. A coastline is where land meets the ocean. But Colombia's coastline is different than most

LEFT: USHUAIA, ARGENTINA

Ushuaia is a city on the southern tip of South America. Because it is south of the Equator, summer and winter are reversed here. January is the warmest month, and June is the coldest.

countries. On one side of the country, the land touches the Pacific Ocean. But on the other side, it touches the Atlantic.

Argentina is much larger than Colombia. It a large and long nation. It stretches north to south for more than two thousand miles. Most people in this country live in large cities. Beyond the cities, you can find large portions of land where only animals live. In the southern part, you can travel for hundreds of miles without seeing another person. A few people live here, but not many.

Another large country is Peru. It sits on the western side of South America. Inside this country, you'll find the great Andes Mountains. The Andes run from the top of South America all the way to the bottom. In fact, the Andes are the longest mountain range in the whole world! The Andes run right through Peru.

On a map, Chile may be the strangest-looking country in the world. It is very long. But it is very narrow. In some ways, it actually does look like a Chili pepper! Chile is 2,600 miles long. But at its widest, it is only 200 miles wide. Because it is so long, it contains many different climates or types of weather. Looking for a hot desert? You can find it in Chile. Looking for snowy tundra? You'll find that in Chile too. Want warm and humid weather? Chile has it.

MAJOR COUNTRIES IN SOUTH AMERICA	
Country	Population
Brazil	213 million
Colombia	51 million
Argentina	45 million
Peru	33 million
Chile	17 million

Llamas in Peru

MOUNTAINS

By awesome deeds in righteousness You will answer us,
O God of our salvation,
You who are the confidence of all the ends of the earth,
And of the far-off seas;
Who established the mountains by His strength,
Being clothed with power. (Psalm 65:5-6)

Mountains teach us about God. They are a picture of how powerful God is. Mountains also remind us of how small we are. They remind us of how big God is too.

Of course, we know that God is much, much bigger than any mountain. To God, the mountains are just a speck of dust. But to us, they are very large.

South America has many tall mountains. The tallest are found in the Andes mountain range.

The tallest mountain in the Americas is Aconcagua. It sits on the border of Argentina and Chile. Climbing such a tall mountain can be very dangerous. For many years, people have tried to reach its summit. (A summit is the top of a mountain.) In 1896, a British man named Edward FitzGerald tried to reach the top. He tried eight times, but he failed each time. It was a Swiss man who reached the summit for the first time. He was a guide named Matthias Zurbriggen. The date was February 13, 1897. Climbing Aconcagua is still treacherous. But many others have done it. In fact, a nine-year-old boy reached the summit in 2013. His name is Tyler Armstrong.

Guanacoes in Patagonia, Chile

OJOS DEL SALADO

Ojos del Salado is the second tallest mountain in South America. It is a volcano, but it hasn't erupted in over 1,000 years.

HIGHEST MOUNTAINS IN SOUTH AMERICA		
Mountain	**Elevation**	**Location**
Aconcagua	22,837 feet	Argentina
Ojos del Salado	22,615 feet	Argentina/Chile
Monte Pissis	22,283 feet	Argentina

RIVERS

You visit the earth and water it,
You greatly enrich it;
The river of God is full of water;
You provide their grain,
For so You have prepared it.
You water its ridges abundantly,
You settle its furrows;
You make it soft with showers,
You bless its growth. (Psalm 65:9-10)

Rivers show us God's goodness. God gave South America a lot of water. It is full of rivers. In the heart of South America, you will find the most impressive river in the world. It is called the Amazon River.

The Amazon contains more water than any other river in the world. It may also be the longest river in the world. It is about the same length as the Nile River in Africa. A trip down the Amazon River will dazzle your eyes with wonder. You will see a rainbow of colors in the plants and animals. Thousands of kinds of birds and fish live here. Thousands of land animals live in this region too.

Such a beautiful place comes with many dangers as well. You might take a swim in the river. But watch out for piranha fish. They might just take a few bites at your arms and legs.

Piranha Fish

Do you like snakes? If so, you should visit the waters of the Amazon. Here you'll find the biggest snake in the world. The green anaconda is the largest snake in the world. It can reach twenty-two feet in length. Get a ruler and measure twenty-two feet. That's a long snake!

When God created the world, He made all things good. But, because sin is in the world, things

Amazon River

THE PARANÁ RIVER

The Paraná River is the second longest river in South America. Many fishermen live on its banks. They make their living catching fish.

have changed. Now many creatures are dangerous. They might hurt or kill us. Thankfully, many of the thousands of creatures in the Amazon are harmless. But no matter how big or small, all of God's creatures teach us about Him. They show us His glory, power, and creativity.

MAJOR RIVERS IN SOUTH AMERICA		
River	Length	Location
Amazon River	4,000 miles	Peru, Colombia, Brazil
Paraná River	3,030 miles	Argentina, Brazil, Paraguay

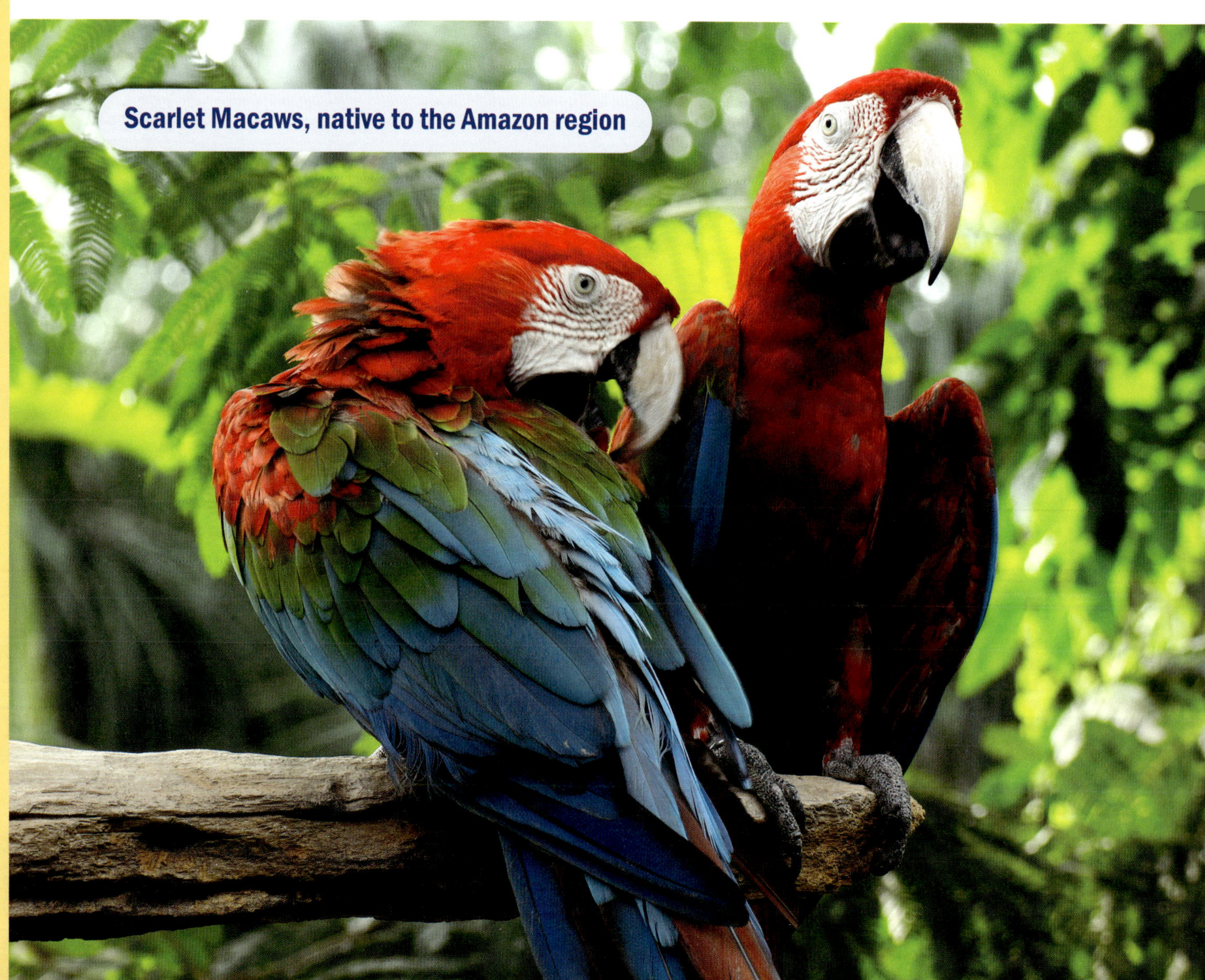

Scarlet Macaws, native to the Amazon region

BEAUTIFUL PLACES

I will extol You, my God, O King;
And I will bless Your name forever and ever.
Every day I will bless You,
And I will praise Your name forever and ever.
Great is the LORD, and greatly to be praised;
And His greatness is unsearchable. (Psalm 145:1-3)

We live on a beautiful planet. Yes, sin has damaged the creation. We see death all over the world. But one day, Jesus will return. One day, He will make all things new. He will conquer death. He will restore His creation. Then we will live in a new heavens and new earth.

Do you think this world is beautiful? It certainly is. But just wait for the next world. It will be even more beautiful.

Let's take a look at some beautiful places in South America. There are many of them!

First, let's stop at Peru. A bus ride and a hike will take you to the top of an ancient city. Machu Picchu sits high in the Andes Mountains. It was built by the Inca peoples long ago. It is 8,000 feet above the ocean. From here, you can see a lovely view of the Andes Mountains. On certain days, you will even be standing higher than the clouds. The Andes truly show us God's power and beauty.

Now let's board a ship from Ecuador and head west. We'll need to sail for 500 miles before we find land. But in time, you'll reach the Galapagos Islands. This is a warm, tropical place. On these islands, you'll find the largest tortoises in the world. This is the only place where they live. The Galapagos giant tortoise can weigh as much as 900 pounds. These creatures

Galapagos Tortoise

Machu Picchu

Perito Moreno Glacier

are slow. They are in no rush. Many of them live until they are one hundred years old. You might also see a marine iguana swimming near the beach. If you are a good swimmer, you can take a dive with the bottlenose dolphins. They swim these waters as well.

After the warm weather on the islands, perhaps you'll want to cool down? Then head down to the southern tip of South America. Here you can visit a glacier. This is where you'll find the Perito Moreno Glacier. It is a giant piece of ice nineteen miles in length. Some of the walls of this glacier are 130 feet tall! Take a stroll on top. But be sure to bring a jacket. The average high in the July winter is 33°.

CENTRAL AMERICA

There is another part of the Americas you should know about. It is called Central America. The countries of Central America are located between Mexico and South America. When compared to North and South America, Central America is quite small. Even though it is small, Central America contains seven countries.

In Panama, ships pass from the Atlantic Ocean to the Pacific Ocean. How do they do this? Ships pass through the Panama Canal. This is a 51-mile-long waterway in Panama. The canal opened in 1914. Since that time, it has made travel much faster for ships. Before the canal opened, ships went south. They would go around the tip of South America. This took much longer. It was also more dangerous. The Panama Canal is very important for shipping around the world.

COUNTRIES IN CENTRAL AMERICA		
Country	**Capital City**	**Population**
Belize	Belmopan	420,000
Costa Rica	San José	5,000,000
El Salvador	San Salvador	6,420,000
Guatemala	Guatemala City	17,200,000
Honduras	Tegucigalpa	9,500,000
Nicaragua	Managua	6,400,000
Panama	Panama City	4,100,000

Note: population totals are approximate.

Panama Canal

PRAYER POINTS: SOUTH AMERICA AND CENTRAL AMERICA

You've now taken a quick tour of South America and Central America. What should you do after seeing all these things? What have we learned about these places? How should we respond?

For the Christian, the first thing we should do is worship God. This should be our natural response. Our hearts should rise up in praise to our great God. Can you see His power and majesty in the beauty of His creation? Take time now to pray a prayer of praise. Let us adore and worship our great God!

- **Praise God for His Power**
  Look at the mighty Amazon River. Then worship the God who stretched out its long waters. Praise the God of power who made the Andes Mountains rise! Surely the God who made all things is mighty! He is mighty to create this world. But He is strong in another way too. He is also mighty to save.

- **Praise God for His Goodness**
  We live in a fallen world. The earth is wounded by the fall into sin. But God is still good to His creation. He gives us water, food, sunshine, warm and cold weather, and more. He is good to the people of South America. He makes the sun rise there every day.

- **Praise God for Beauty**
  Our God is creative with His art. He uses many colors. He skillfully draws mountains, forests, rivers, glaciers. He makes beautiful sights for us to look at. Our God creates wondrous and beautiful animals. Let us praise Him for His beauty and creativity.

Mesa Verde National Park, Colorado

THE AMERICAS BEFORE CHRIST

3

Do you have a globe of the earth in your home? If you do, go get it. With your finger, find North and South America. Now look to the left of the Americas. What's there? Next, look to the right. What do you see to the west and east of this landmass?

If you said, "lots of blue," you're right. Two huge oceans fill the space on either side of the Americas. To the west is the Pacific. To the east is the Atlantic. These two oceans separate this land from the rest of the world.

Perhaps this makes you wonder. If this land is so far away from everything else, how did people get here?

In this book, you will learn about people who came to explore the Americas. When they arrived, they found other people living here. There were already many people groups living in this part of the world.

So how did all these people groups get to America? And how long ago did they come here?

NOAH'S FLOOD AND THE TOWER OF BABEL

The Bible is God's Word. Everything the Bible tells us is true. If we want to understand history, we need to read the Bible. It tells us what happened long ago. It teaches us the earliest history of the world.

The first book of the Bible is called Genesis. Chapter 1 of Genesis tells us how God created the world.

A few chapters later, the first man and woman sin against God. Adam and Eve ate the fruit God told them not to. This brought sin and misery to the world. From then on, the earth would be filled with sin.

But God promised to fix the problem of sin. He promised to send a Redeemer. Later in the Bible, we find out who the Redeemer is. He is Jesus Christ. Through Jesus, peoples of every tribe, tongue, and nation would be saved.

After Adam and Eve left the garden, they had children. Then their children had children. More and more people lived on the earth. But they also became more and more evil. Violence and wickedness filled the earth. Adam and Eve's sin changed the world forever. Sin brought misery and death into the world.

With sorrow, God said, "I will destroy the world." Then the Lord sent a flood. Water covered the whole earth. The flood washed away the wicked. It killed the evil people. But the Lord didn't kill all people. He chose Noah and his family to survive the flood. Through Noah's family, the world would be filled with people again.

After the flood, God told Noah to be fruitful and multiply. He wanted Noah's family to have many children. He wanted them to fill the earth with people.

Noah and his family

Tower of Babel

Noah had three sons. Every person on earth came from these three sons. Their names were Shem, Ham, and Japheth. The children of Noah should have spread across the earth. But instead, they rebelled. Many people banded together. They made a plan to "make a name" for themselves. They decided to build a tower to reach the heavens. But God did not want them all to stay in one place. He wanted them to fill the earth. God commanded Noah to take dominion. He wanted Noah and his sons to rule over the earth and fill it with people.

The Lord stopped the tower that the people were trying to build. He confused the languages of the builders. Now they couldn't understand each other. Then the Lord scattered them all over the world. People left Babel and spread across the entire globe. They began to fill the earth.

NATIVES OF THE AMERICAS

These were the families of the sons of Noah, according to their generations, in their nations; and from these the nations were divided on the earth after the flood. (Genesis 10:32)

After the people left Babel, they began to fill the earth. Sometime after this, descendants of Noah's sons arrived in the Americas. We don't know when these first people arrived. And we're not quite sure how they got here. The Bible doesn't tell us how this happened. To find out, we have to look at other history.

People who study history are called **historians**. They try to figure out what happened in the past. An **archaeologist** studies history too. They search for clues about how people lived long, long ago. Then they decide what they think happened. Sometimes they're right. But sometimes they're wrong. The Bible is the only perfect record of history. It always tells us the truth. Other history books make mistakes. They might not be correct in what they say.

Historian

A person who studies history. They help us understand what happened in the past. The Bible is the only perfect history book. We should use this when we study history. It always tells us the truth.

Archaeologist

Someone who studies human history. They do this by digging. They dig up old objects from the past. By studying these things, they learn about what people were like long ago.

How did the first people reach America? Some think they crossed the sea from Asia. The Pacific Ocean is very large. It's difficult and dangerous to cross. But one part of Asia almost touches America. The eastern tip of Russia is only fifty-one miles from Alaska. This would be an easy place to sail across.

Thousands of years ago, this part of the ocean might have been dry. There might have been a land bridge here. Then people could have walked across to Alaska.

But even if there was water, it would be easy to cross in boats. By boat, people could have landed in Alaska. They could also have sailed down the coast into the rest of America. From the coast, these

Archaeologist uncovering bones

The Bering Strait
The Bering Strait separates the Americas from Asia. Only fifty-one miles separate Russia from Alaska.

people could have gone deeper inland.

Or perhaps the first Americans came from somewhere else. The Greeks, Romans, Egyptians, and others were very good at sailing ships. Maybe some of them crossed the Atlantic Ocean. It seems amazing to us that they could have traveled so far across the ocean. But ancient peoples had wisdom and great skill. They were very smart and did many surprising things. It is possible they crossed the ocean. But we don't know for sure.

Satellite image of the Bering Strait

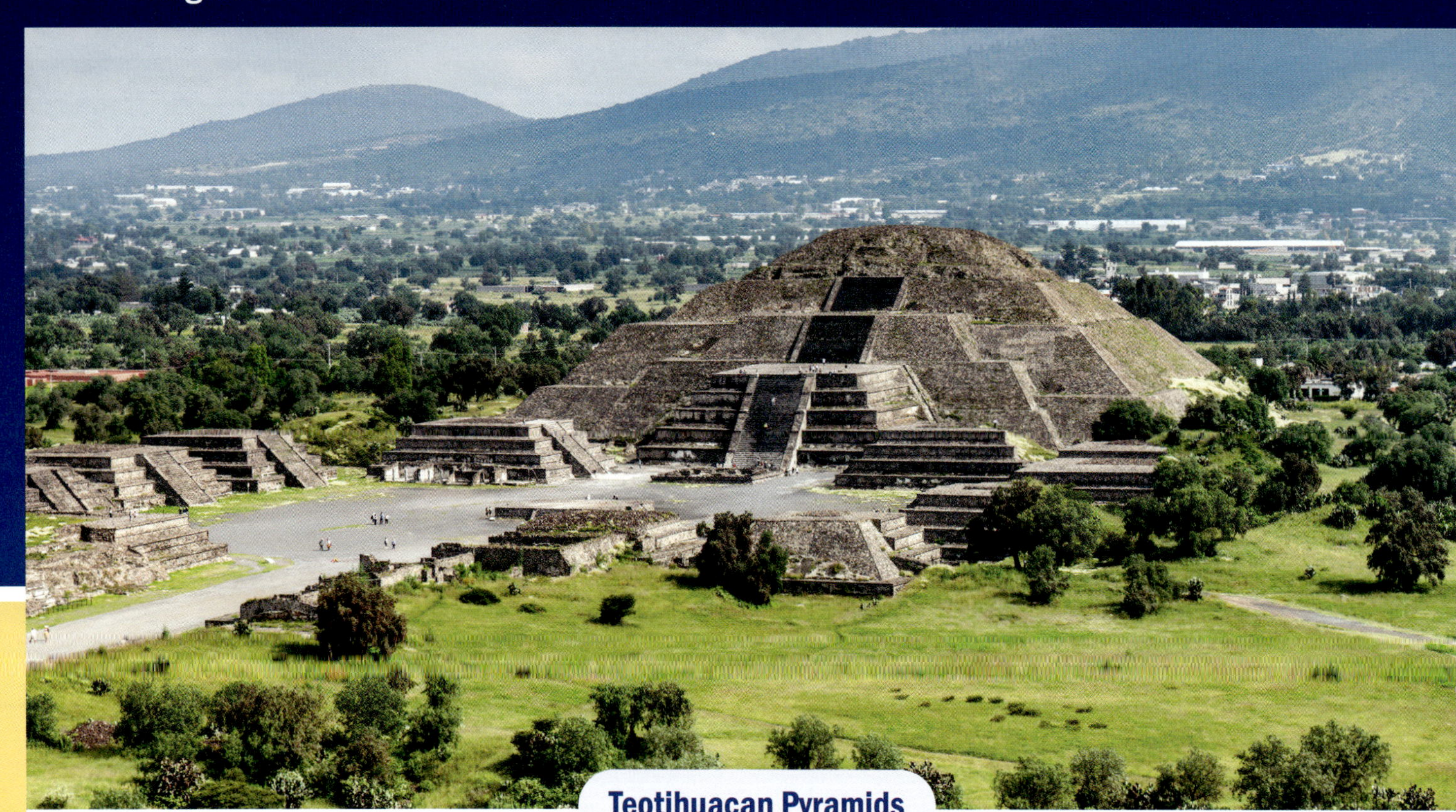

Teotihuacan Pyramids

PEOPLES OF MEXICO AND SOUTH AMERICA

What is man that You are mindful of him,
And the son of man that You visit him?
For You have made him a little lower than the angels,
And You have crowned him with glory and honor.
You have made him to have dominion over the works of Your hands;
You have put all things under his feet. (Psalm 8:4-6)

Let's learn more about the early peoples of America. These people are gone. They died many, many years ago. But many things they built still remain.

What do we know about natives in Mexico and South America? What kind of people lived here?

Near Mexico City, you can find many old buildings. These are from the Aztec Empire. The Aztec people lived around AD 1400-1600. Most of their houses and homes are gone. But many ziggurats they built still survive. Take a look at the picture on the previous page. Ziggurats look a little like Egyptian pyramids. They also look like ziggurats found in Babylon. One of the largest of these ziggurats is named the Pyramid of the Sun. Long ago, it probably had a temple at the top of it. The temple no longer stands. But the ziggurat does.

The Aztec people worshiped the things God created. They did not worship the one true God. They didn't know about the only Savior Jesus. Their false gods could not save them. One day, though, the Aztecs would learn about the true God.

The Aztecs lived near Mexico. Around the same time, another empire ruled in the south. This was the Inca Empire. It ruled over a large part of South America. For a time, it stretched across most of the continent. The Inca Empire was massive!

The Incas also did not worship the one true God. They didn't know that Jesus was Savior of the world. They were a sinful nation. But, like all humans of the world, the Incas were made in God's image. We are all made in the image of God. This means we have knowledge, and we know about God and about right and wrong. It also means God created us to take dominion of the earth. We should take care of the earth and rule over it. God also wants us to be holy just as He is holy. The Incas were not a holy people. They were a wicked, sinful people. But they were smart and skillful.

The Incas were skilled at many things. They planted farms. They were good at math and astronomy. They were also very good at building things. In 1911, an American found an ancient Inca site. It was high up in the Andes Mountains. It is called Machu Picchu. Long ago, this might have been a home for one of the Inca rulers. It is almost 8,000 feet above sea level. One of the amazing things about this city is the stonework in it. The Incas were skilled engineers. They knew how to make stone buildings that would last for hundreds of years.

Many buildings in Machu Picchu are built with large, heavy stones. The Incas carefully cut these stones to fit together. They didn't use mortar or cement. Instead, they carefully polished the stones. Each stone fits together almost perfectly. Even today, these stones stand strong where the Incas built them. The Incas also created roads in and out of Machu Picchu. Many of the stone roads they built still exist today.

Machu Picchu shows us how smart people can be. Sadly, sin has brought much evil to the world. Yes, people are full of sin. All humans need a Redeemer. But the image of God still shines in all people, even though they sin.

In Peru, we find one other strange thing that people made long ago. Near the coast of Peru, you will find the **Nazca lines**. These are lines drawn in the desert. The lines form shapes or drawings. There are thousands of drawings etched into the ground. Here you can find the shapes of many animals. Fish, spiders, hummingbirds, and lizards are all here. Some drawings are of human beings. If you're standing on the ground, you can't see the whole shape. Instead, you have to go up in an airplane to see the drawing. People made the lines by digging small trenches in the ground. The trenches are about 4 to 6 inches deep. Why did people make these lines? We don't know. But these lines show us how smart

Terraces at Machu Picchu

Stonework at Machu Picchu

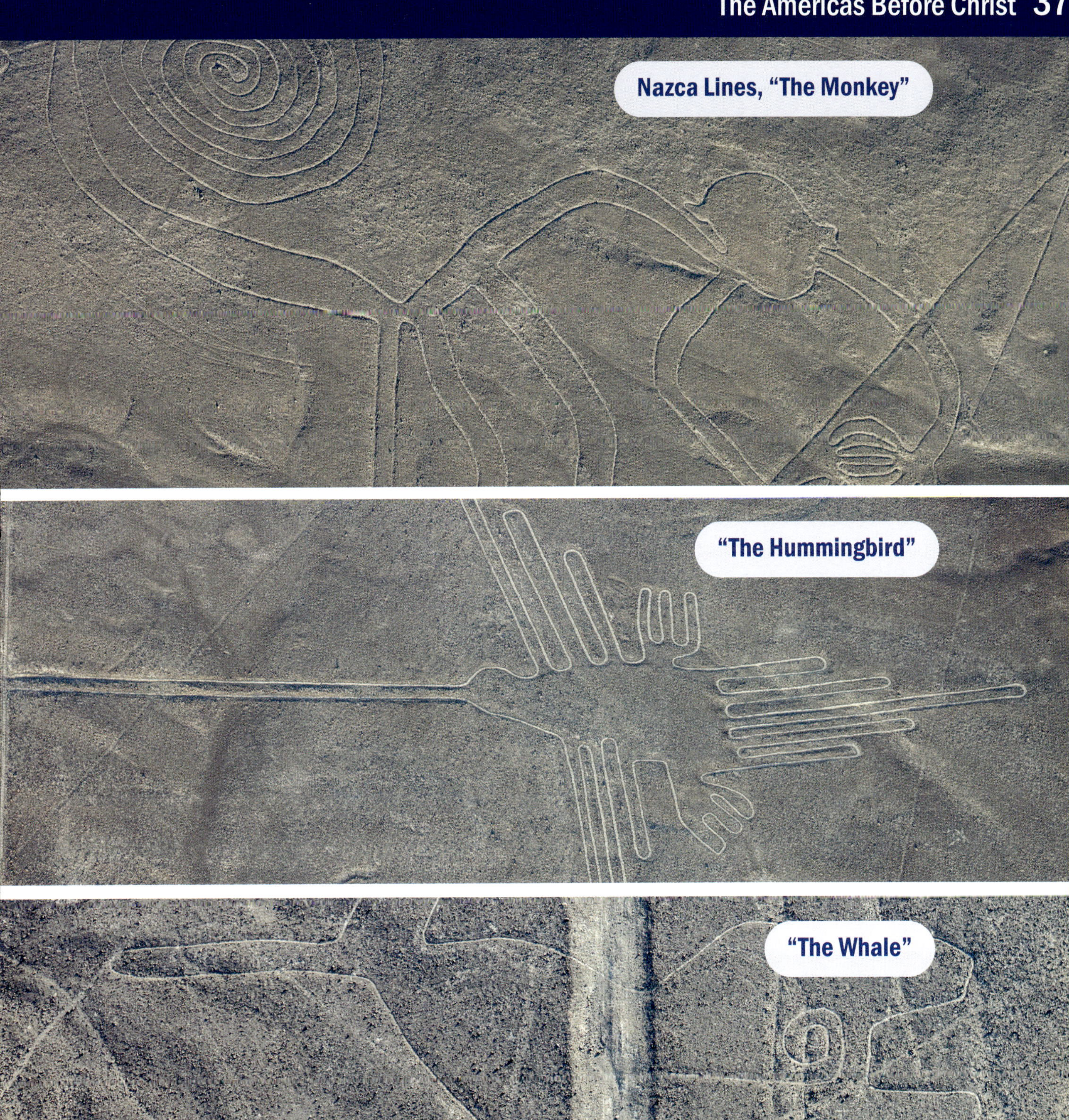

the peoples of South America were. It took a lot of work and skill to make these huge shapes and drawings.

PEOPLES OF NORTH AMERICA

"We are bringing you good news. Turn away from these worthless things. Turn to the living God. He is the one who made the heavens and the earth and the sea. He made everything in them. In the past, he let all nations go their own way. But he has given proof of what he is like. He has shown kindness by giving you rain from heaven. He gives you crops in their seasons. He provides you with plenty of food. He fills your hearts with joy." (Acts 14:15-17 NIRV)

Let's look next at North America. Here, we find many people groups that were very large. We don't know much about these people. But we know that some of the tribes were nomadic. This means they were always moving from one place to another. They didn't live in one place like we do. These tribes usually got their food by hunting. They didn't farm or plant gardens. To grow food, you have to stay in one place and work the land. Instead, these tribes moved from place to place. They went wherever there were animals to hunt.

Some tribes did have farms, though. Many of these people lived in the southwestern part of the continent. Today, this land is part of four states. They are Colorado, New Mexico, Arizona, and Utah. The Anasazi Indians had farms and raised crops. But their homes were not the same as ours. They lived

Monks Mound

Cliff dwellings

high up in cliffs. You can still see these amazing houses today. Go sometime and visit the Four Corners. At the Four Corners, you can touch four states at the same time. Near there, you can see many old homes in the cliffs.

In some places in the United States, you can find huge earth mounds. These mounds were built by many tribes. We don't know why some of them were built. But we think the mounds are very old. One mound, called Poverty Point, was built around 1200 BC. It is about seventy-five feet tall.

Monks Mound is in the state of Illinois. It is 100 feet tall, 1,000 feet long, and 775 feet wide. At its base, it is about the same size as the Great Pyramid in Egypt. The natives who made this mound brought soil and clay to build it. It must have been a big project!

Like the Incas, the natives of North America were smart. They were intelligent. They were also creative. They built cities. They planted farms. They started settlements. Even though they were filled with sin, they still had God's image in them.

It's good to be smart. But the Bible tells us that we can't be saved by being smart. If we don't know Jesus, we are "without hope and without God in the world" (Eph. 2:12). The peoples in America built many huge things. They were skilled at what they did. But they didn't have any hope. They didn't know the true God. One day, this would change. One day, these natives would learn about Jesus, the Savior of the world.

Viking Ship

4

LEIF ERIKSON AND THE VIKINGS

Those who go down to the sea in ships,
Who do business on great waters,
They see the works of the LORD,
And His wonders in the deep. (Psalm 107:23-24)

Leif peered over the bow of the ship. Ninety feet long with a dragon's head, the Viking ship was an impressive sight.

"Land! Land!" cried one of the sailors.

In the distance, an icy coast was spotted. The Vikings had discovered a new island. It was the island we know today as Greenland.

Leif was just a boy when he first saw Greenland. He and his family had embarked for the west. As Vikings, they had lived in Iceland. But Leif's father Erik the Red ran into legal troubles there. He was outlawed from the island. Erik could have returned to Norway. Or he could have taken his family to Ireland or Scotland. But instead, Eric wanted freedom. Together with his family, he set sail for the west.

Some thought Erik was crazy. Was there any land west of Iceland? Or would Erik and his family die at sea? No one knew.

Around the year 982, Erik the Red reached Greenland. The voyage took many weeks. Around fifty people were with him in the ship. Wearily, they set foot on the newfound island.

The sight of Greenland dazzled their senses. It was a much greener land than Iceland. The land was full of creatures too. Whales, seals, and walruses filled the waters. Foxes and caribou roamed the land. With all these animals, Erik and his family would never lack food. The Norse settlers also

"Summer in the Greenland Coast" by Carl Rasmussen

found polar bears. The fur of these beautiful creatures would soon keep their new homes warm.

Erik and his family started a colony on the island. They called it Brattahlid. For the next few years, they lived here and explored the rest of Greenland.

Three years later, Erik returned to Iceland. He told other Icelanders about Greenland. It was Erik who named it Greenland. He said, "This name of Greenland will draw other Norse to join me there."

Erik was right. Twenty-five ships returned with him to Greenland in AD 986.

KING OLAF OF NORWAY

Yes, all kings shall fall down before Him;
All nations shall serve Him. (Psalm 72:11)

Leif shared his father Erik's love for exploration. He often stared at the ocean, wondering what lay beyond. Leif wanted to go further west. Perhaps he could find more land, a new land that no one had ever found before.

Leif went to his father and asked him for a ship.

"Father, I would like a ship. I want to sail west and explore."

Erik said, "Very well. I will give you a ship. But first, you must sail east, not west. Return to our homeland of Norway. You must visit the king. Tell him about Greenland. Take him gifts from our beautiful land."

Leif agreed to what his father asked of him. Leif said, "Father, I will go to Norway. But then I will sail west of Greenland. I will sail into new waters where no one has gone before."

Erik gave Leif his ship. Leif and the other Norsemen prepared for their long journey. The ship was loaded with walrus hides, skins, and ropes. These were gifts for the king of Norway. Then Leif chose a special present for the king. He captured a Greenland polar bear. Such an impressive gift was just right for the great king of Norway.

Leif set sail for Norway. It was around the year AD 998. Before reaching Norway, Leif and his companions stopped on the Orkney Islands. Here, earlier Vikings had settled and lived. Today, the Orkney Islands are part of Scotland.

Model of Viking Ship

After a long and perilous journey, Leif reached the shores of Norway. He was welcomed into the court of King Olaf.

King Olaf was delighted by Leif's gifts. He thanked Leif for the polar bear and the other treasures from Greenland.

King Olaf asked Leif, "Are you a Christian?"

Leif answered, "No, O king. I am not."

King Olaf explained to Leif his plans for Norway. "I am a Christian, Leif. I want the Christian faith to spread through all of Norway. I would like you and the others in Greenland to become Christians as well."

King Olaf make Erik the Red the ruler of Greenland. He told Leif that he would be ruler after his father. The king also asked Leif, "Will you take two Christian teachers with you? Will you take Christianity to Greenland?"

Leif knew his father did not like Christians. But he agreed to King Olaf's request.

Leif and his companions stayed in King Olaf's court for some months. During this time, Leif became a Christian. He was baptized in the name of the Father, Son, and Holy Spirit. Now, Leif wanted his family to become followers of Jesus Christ.

Icebergs in Greenland

Leif returned to Greenland. Erik was proud of all the things his son had done. But Erik was not interested in becoming a Christian. He believed in the Norse gods. He didn't want to learn about the true God.

However, Leif's mother did become a Christian. Thjodhild received the Word and was baptized. But this angered Erik. He was so angry that he didn't speak to his wife for a month. Leif spoke to his father and tried to make peace. At last, Erik agreed to accept his wife again. But he still did not become a Christian.

LEIF DISCOVERS NORTH AMERICA

By awesome deeds in righteousness You will answer us,
O God of our salvation,
You who are the confidence of all the ends of the earth,
And of the far-off seas. (Psalm 65:5)

Shortly after he returned to Greenland, Leif left again. Preparing his ship, he left on his next journey. It was time to sail west into the unknown.

Leif had a friend who had seen land to the west of Greenland. His friend's name was Bjarni. The land he saw may have been the coast of modern-day Canada. This gave Leif hope. Perhaps there was land to be found.

It was the year 1000. Leif and his fellow Greenlanders set sail.

After days of sailing the frigid waters of the North Atlantic, Leif spotted land. It was a barren, rocky shore. Leif and his companions went ashore.

Where were they? We think Leif first landed in modern-day Newfoundland and Labrador. Today, this land is part of Canada. Leif Erikson was the first Christian to ever reach the Americas.

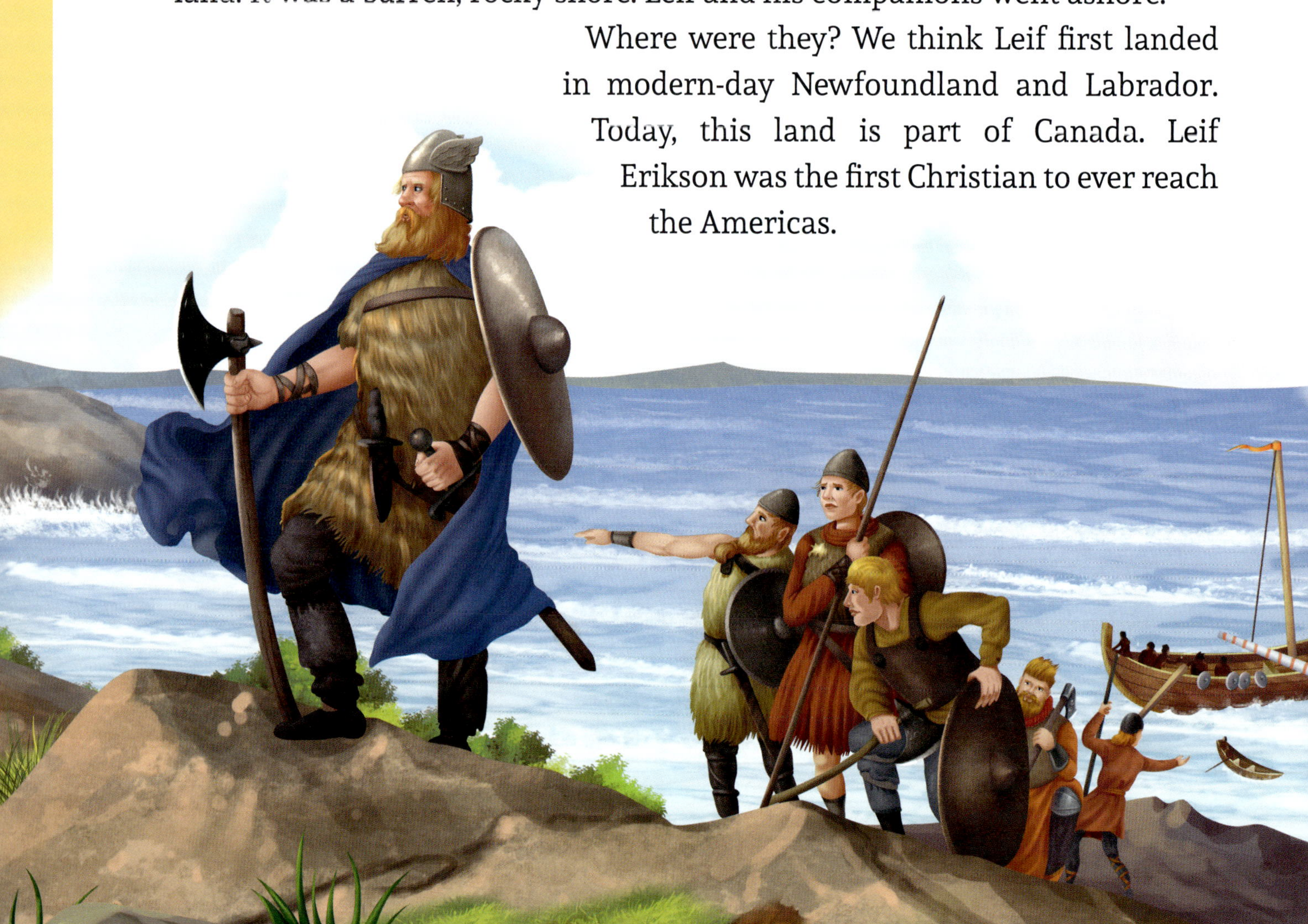

"Bjarni was right!" Leif exclaimed. "There is land here."

Leif and his men decided to keep exploring. They followed the coastline of Labrador south. They crossed the Gulf of St. Lawrence. Leif was stunned by the beauty of this land. Here was a land greener than Greenland!

Leif and the Greenlanders built a settlement. The land was filled with animals and plant life. And the weather was better too. The winters here weren't as cold as they were in Greenland.

Spring arrived. Warm weather came. The Norsemen gathered timber and grew grapes. Leif named the new land "Vineland." It was called Vineland because Leif grew grapes there.

LATER EXPLORERS

Leif returned to Greenland with the good news. There was beautiful and rich land to the west!

When Leif arrived in Greenland, his brother Thorvald came out to meet him. "Leif, our father has died."

News of his father's death filled Leif with sadness. But now it was his job to care for the colony. Leif became the leader of Brattahlid.

Soon, a church was built in Greenland. It was the first Christian church on the island.

Leif's home was Greenland. This was where he lived. But he still wanted to find out more about the lands to the west. He wanted someone to explore this new part of the world. His brother Thorvald set sail next. He again reached the new world. He even went further south than Leif had gone. Thorvald likely reached the region of New England.

In 1003, a man named Thorfinn came to Greenland. He married a woman named Gudrid. Leif told Thorfinn that he should settle in Vineland in the new world.

One hundred and thirty people left Greenland in AD 1004. They set sail for Vineland. When they arrived, they started a new colony there. They hoped to start a permanent settlement in the new land.

But their plans didn't work out. The Norse ran into trouble with the native Eskimos. Thorfinn decided it was not safe to stay in Vineland. He and the others got back in their ship and returned to Greenland.

The Vikings never forgot about Vineland. They wrote down the stories of Erik the Red and Leif Erikson. They wrote about Thorfinn too.

In the 1960s, someone found an ancient settlement in Canada. They found old Norse buildings and tools on the coast of Newfoundland. It looks like about one hundred Norse people used to live here. Here is a sign that the Norse did visit North America.

Leif was the first Christian to visit North America. By God's grace, he would not be the last.

Statue of Thorfinn

Reconstructed Viking Hall in Newfoundland, Canada

Coast of Newfoundland

5 CHRISTOPHER COLUMBUS: REACHING THE NEW WORLD

The LORD has made bare His holy arm
In the eyes of all the nations;
And all the ends of the earth shall see
The salvation of our God. (Isaiah 52:10)

"Land! Land!" shouted Rodrigo de Triana.

Aboard the Pinta, the sailor had spotted an island on the horizon. It was 2:00 AM on October 12, 1492.

It was true. The sailors saw a flickering light in the distance. After four weeks at sea, the Niña, Pinta, and Santa Maria had reached land.

Four long weeks had passed since the ships left Spain. The sailors were tired, hungry, and afraid. They had spent many days worrying. Would they ever spot land? Or would they run out of food in the middle of the ocean? What would happen then?

The answer came that morning.

After the sun rose, Christopher Columbus and his men dropped anchor. Then they climbed into three small boats and rowed to shore.

Filled with relief, the men felt firm ground under their feet at last. In joy they fell to their knees. Columbus gave thanks to God. The Lord had brought the men and their ships safely across the ocean. Columbus wept tears of joy. Then he named the island they were standing on. He called it "San Salvador." In Spanish, this means "Holy Savior." Columbus knew that God had protected him and his men. God was the One who had brought them safely to land.

Columbus thought he had landed in Asia. But he was wrong. He had sailed west to find Asia. Instead, he was in the Americas. He had discovered this new land by mistake.

COLUMBUS SAILS FROM SPAIN

Why did Christopher Columbus sail west? He tells us why in his own writings. As a child, Columbus read the Bible. In the Bible, God talks about sending His Word to the whole world. Jesus Christ is Lord of the whole earth, and He wants all people to learn about Him. Columbus wondered, "How will the world hear about God? Who will teach the people in other parts of the world? How will they learn God's Word?" When he grew up, Columbus decided that he wanted to go to far-off places. He would bring God's Word with him. He wanted to find a way to sail to Asia. He would bring the Christian faith to that country.

People in Europe already knew how to get to Asia. They sailed in ships all the way down the long coast of Africa. After they passed the tip of Africa, they turned north and sailed toward the Indies. Finally, they reached Asia after a long, hard journey. But Columbus wanted to find an easier way. He wanted to bring the gospel to the Indies, so he thought of a faster way to get there.

Christopher Columbus

"If I sail west from Europe, I could reach the Indies more quickly," he said.

Columbus knew the earth was round. People had believed this for a long time. Because the earth is round, Columbus knew he could sail one way and reach the other side of the world.

But Columbus didn't know how big the earth was. How long would it take to sail around the world and reach Asia? He also didn't know about the Americas. He thought he could sail straight across the ocean all the way to Asia. He thought the rest of the earth was covered in water, not land.

Many people said Columbus was crazy to make such a voyage. "You're a fool!" they cried. "The ocean is much larger than you think! You will never make it to Asia. You will die before you get there."

But Columbus wasn't scared. "Not so!" he said. "We could reach Asia in two or three weeks." He was sure he was right. But he had one problem. He needed money for the trip.

Columbus didn't have enough money to buy ships for his voyage. He needed a patron to pay for the ships. But a patron wasn't easy to find. For years, he searched for someone to help him. At last, in January 1492, a king and queen agreed to assist him. King Ferdinand and Queen Isabella of Spain said yes. They would pay for the ships. They would also buy food for the sailors and men on the voyage.

King Ferdinand

Queen Isabella

Patron

Someone who gives money and help to a person or cause.

Niña, Pinta, and Santa Maria

In August 1492, the Niña, Pinta, and Santa Maria set sail from Spain. This was a very risky journey. But Columbus believed in the mission.

WHY DID CHRISTOPHER COLUMBUS GO?

I will also give You as a light to the Gentiles,
That You should be My salvation to the ends of the earth. (Isaiah 49:6)

Why did Christopher Columbus sail west? What was he looking for?

In his journals, Columbus tells us why he went. He wanted to spread God's Word to the ends of the earth. "The Bible says that Jesus will bring salvation to the ends of the earth," he said. "I want to spread God's glory across the world."

People in Asia didn't know about God. Columbus wanted to teach them. He wanted to go to the Indies to bring God's Word to the people there. He wrote, "By reading the Scriptures, I was inspired to find a way to the Indies."

Columbus firmly believed that the Bible was God's Word. He said: "Jesus

Columbus lands on San Salvador

said all things will pass away. But not His marvelous Word. Therefore, I hold to the authority of the Holy Scriptures."

"It was the Lord who gave me the desire to sail to the Indies. The gospel must be preached to every land. But who will preach it? Someone must go. That is what convinced me. I knew that we must travel across the seas to fulfill Christ's Great Commission."

MEETING THE NATIVES

When Columbus found America, he thought he was in the Indies. He was filled with joy. "We have reached the Indies!" he cried. But he was actually a very long way from Asia!

Even though he was in the wrong land, this was part of God's plan. The Lord had planned this trip. When Columbus found America, the whole world changed.

Soon after landing, the Spanish met natives on the island. Columbus called them "Indians." He called them this because he thought he was in the Indies. The name "Indian" has stuck ever since. Even today, many native Americans are called Indians.

The natives spoke to Columbus and his men. Columbus didn't know what they were saying, so he used sign language. The natives used hand signals back. By talking like this, Columbus learned there were other islands nearby.

For the next few weeks, he explored other islands. Then he sailed back to Spain.

RETURN TO SPAIN AND LATER JOURNEYS

On March 15, 1493, Columbus reached Spain. His ships shot off a gunfire salute. Joy filled the men. Large crowds gathered at the port to meet them. Everyone was excited to hear what Columbus had found. They held feasts in his honor.

Columbus met with the king and queen. He told them about the land he had found.

"O king and queen, I must tell you about the Indies. It is a beautiful land.

Columbus returns to Spain

The natives there are innocent and gentle. There are also incredible riches to be found there. See this gold necklace. Here is a beautiful bird from the Indies as well. Let us take more ships to the Indies!"

King Ferdinand and Queen Isabella were amazed. They agreed to pay for more voyages. In all, Columbus made three more trips to the Americas.

The Spanish people started colonies on some of the islands. But many of these colonies did not last. The people ran out of food. Then they died of famine and sickness. Wars also started between the Spanish and the natives.

Sadly, some of the Spanish treated the Indians badly. They made some of the people slaves. Some Spanish men said, "This will be good for the natives. We can teach them to become Christians." But this was wrong.

Some Spanish came to find gold. They didn't care about the natives. They didn't care about God's Word either. They only cared about themselves and about getting rich.

GOD HAD A PLAN

Christopher Columbus wanted to do good in the Indies. He wanted to bring the Christian faith to that land.

He wrote, "I prayed to the most merciful Lord. I told Him my heart's desire. This was my goal. I wanted to see the Christian faith spread."

After four voyages, Columbus returned to Spain. He died in 1506. Before his death, he prayed one last prayer to God. He knew that Jesus Christ is the only One who can save sinners. Columbus was a sinner, but he trusted that God would keep His promise. God would save him just like He promised in His Word. Columbus prayed: "Into Your hands, O Lord, I commend my spirit." Then he died.

Columbus never knew that he discovered the Americas. He still thought he had sailed to the Indies.

The Bible says, "A man's heart plans his way, but the Lord directs his steps." Columbus planned to go to the Indies. Instead, he went to America by accident. But this was exactly what God had planned. God is sovereign over all. He had a purpose for Columbus. He had a plan for America. Soon, many more people would come to this new land. They would start colonies there too.

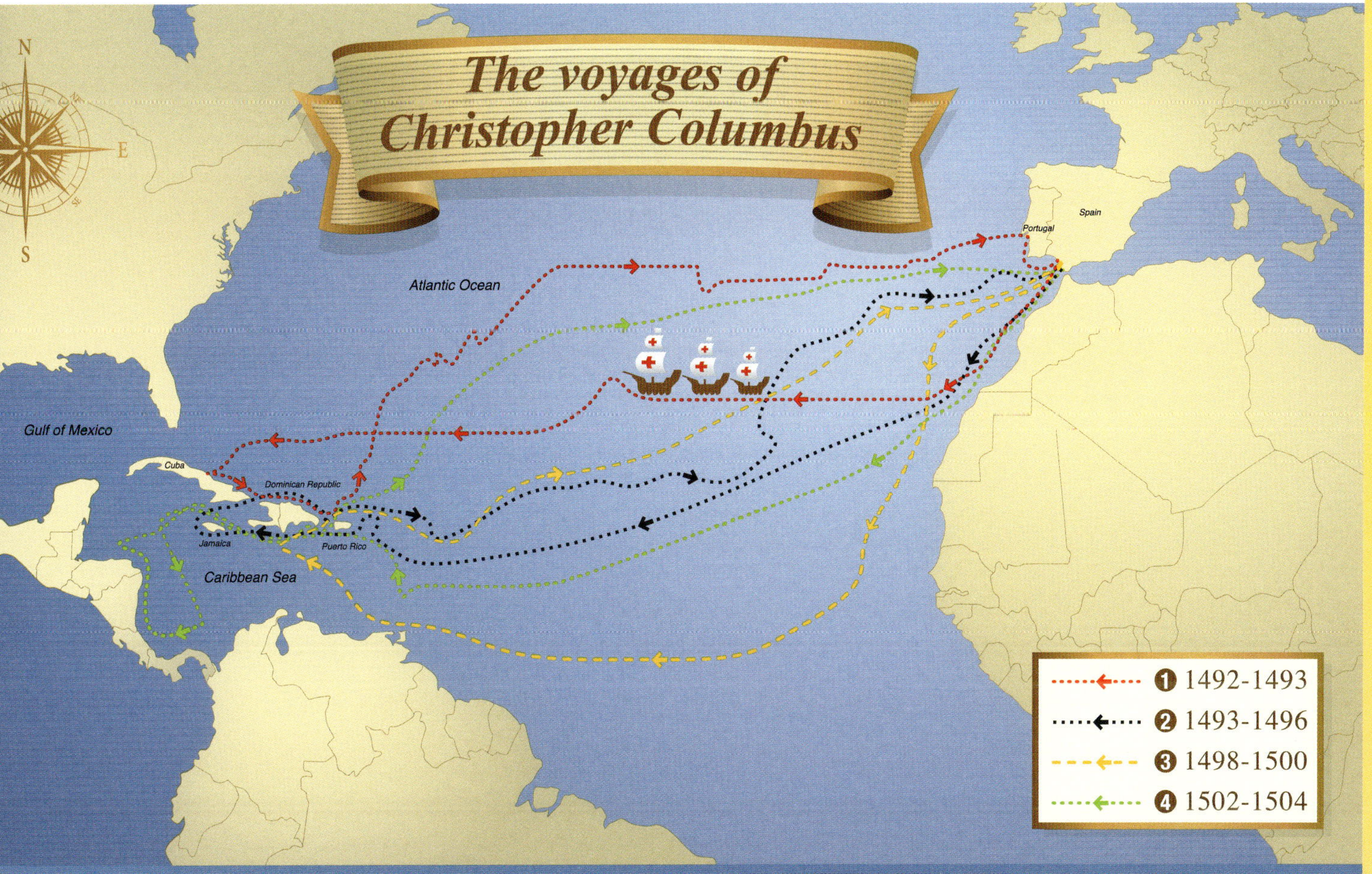

Wicked men would do evil things in the Americas. But God's people would also come. God's people would bring the good news of Jesus.

A new day dawned in the Americas. Soon, the light of Jesus Christ would shine in that dark land.

"I am the light of the world. He who follows Me shall not walk in darkness, but have the light of life." (John 8:12)

Trunk Bay, St. John

Monte Alban, Mexico

6 THE CONQUISTADORS

When Christopher Columbus returned to Spain, he brought tales of his adventures with him. The new world was an enchanting place. Amazed, the Spanish listened. They were filled with wonder by his tales. Soon other men wanted to visit this strange new land. The king of Spain was glad to help them. He hoped this new world would bring riches to his kingdom.

King Ferdinand II encouraged men to go to the new world. He promised to support those who were willing to go. The journey was long. The risks were many. But there were riches to be had. Many men decided to take the risk. The king agreed to sponsor some of them. But the men had to agree to the king's terms. Twenty percent of all profits from the journey went to the king. This was called "the king's royal fifth." (A fifth is the same as twenty percent.)

The king gave rewards to any man brave enough to go to the new world. If an explorer conquered some land there, he had to give it to the king. But the king let the explorer settle there. He would then become the governor of this new land. He would rule over it for the king.

One of the first to embark was a man named Vasco de Balboa. He made several trips to America. On one of these trips, he found the Pacific Ocean. He was the first man from Europe to see it from the new world. This happened in 1513. Balboa explored the region of Panama for two months. He found gold there. With this exciting news, he returned to Spain. Gold was worth a lot of money, and it was very rare. It wasn't easy to find in Europe. Because of this, many Spaniards wanted to go to the new world. They hoped to find vast wealth there.

Vasco de Balboa (1475-1519)

Soon, more men made their way across the Atlantic. Some came to bring the gospel to the new world. They wanted the natives to know about Jesus Christ. Others were looking for earthly riches. Some wanted both.

A Spaniard named Ponce de Leon came next. In 1513, he explored the island of Puerto Rico. From the Indians, Ponce de Leon heard of a land filled with gold. He never found this land. But he did discover Florida. He built a colony there. He called it St. Augustine. You can still visit St. Augustine in Florida today. Some of the old Spanish forts and houses are still there. It is the oldest European settlement in North America.

Ponce de Leon (1474-1521)

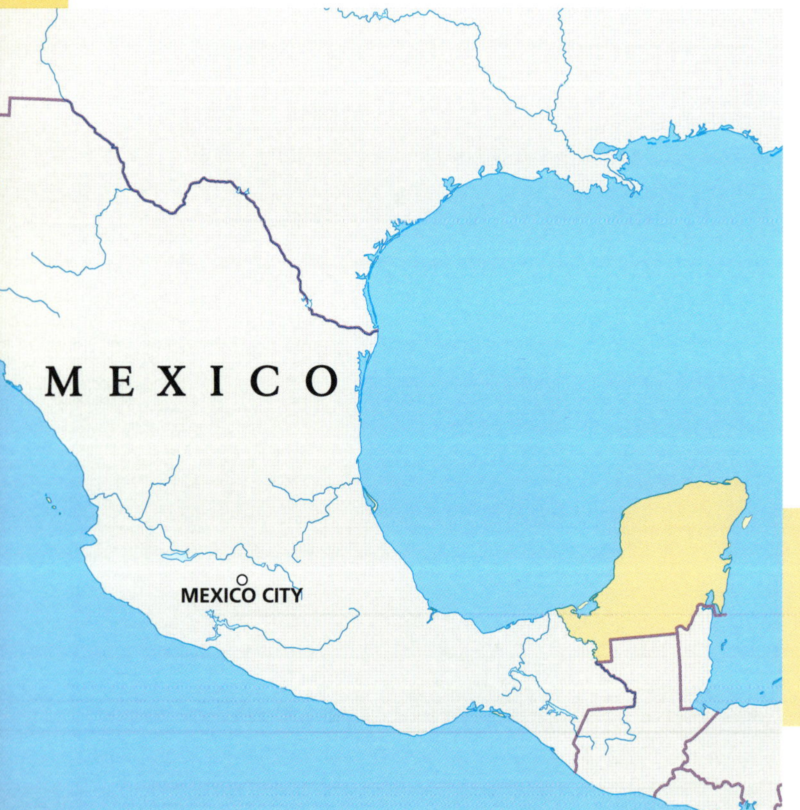

HERNANDO CORTES CONQUERS THE AZTECS

At this time, the Aztec people lived in southern Mexico. Their empire was large and strong. They built many cities on the **Yucatan Peninsula**. Hernando Cortes decided to explore this region.

Definition: **Peninsula**

A piece of land mostly surrounded by water.

Cortes and his men left Cuba and made landfall on the peninsula. The Spanish soon met natives there. They were adorned with golden jewelry. Cortes' men asked him, "Where do these people come from? Where did they get this gold? We must find out!"

The Indians told the Spaniards where they got the jewelry. "You must go west into the mountains. The Aztecs live there. It is a land with much gold."

Cortes went back to Cuba. He wanted to find this gold. But he needed supplies and soldiers. If he wanted to conquer the Aztecs, he had to be ready for a fight. He took with him many fighting men. In Spanish, these men were called Conquistadors. This is a big word that means "conqueror."

Why did Cortes go to the Aztecs? One of his men explained their mission. Bernal Diaz del Castillo said, "We came here to serve God and also get rich." The Spanish took the Christian faith to the new world. But their love of money often got in the way. The Bible says that the love of money is the root of all kinds of evil (1 Tim. 6:10).

By 1519, Cortes' army was ready. He had filled eleven ships with supplies. One hundred sailors manned the vessels. Five hundred soldiers stood ready. These were the men Cortes would lead ashore. On February 10, 1519, Cortes' forces left Cuba. Before setting sail, Cortes urged his men, "Friends, let us follow the cross. With true faith in this symbol, we will conquer."

Illustration of Aztec Temple

Hernando Cortes (1485-1547)

When he landed, Cortes did battle with the local Indians. There were far more Indians than Spaniards. But the Spaniards had horses. The natives had never seen horses before. They were afraid of these strange new beasts. They were too scared to fight them.

The natives quickly surrendered. As a peace offering, they gave gifts to the Spaniards. These gifts were jewelry and food. They also gave slaves to Cortes and his men. One of the slaves was a girl named Malinali. She was the first of the natives to become a Christian. She learned Spanish. Then she became an interpreter for the Spaniards.

The Spaniards marched to the capital city of the Aztecs. It was the great city of Tenochtitlan (pronounced "te-nosh-tit-lan"). Natives ran ahead to the city. They warned the people about Cortes. "Invaders are coming!" they cried.

The news reached Montezuma. He was the ruler of the Aztec Empire. Montezuma sent gifts to Cortes. He hoped to have peace with the Spanish.

After a journey of some weeks, Cortes and his men entered Tenochtitlan. They were amazed as they looked at the city. The Aztec Empire was a sight to behold. Montezuma welcomed Cortes to the great city. For a time, there was peace between the Aztecs and the Spanish.

The city was filled with beauty. But Cortes soon learned about a dark evil. The Aztecs worshiped false gods. They believed in human sacrifice. Day by day, they killed many human beings. Pagan priests murdered them. They did this to worship their false gods.

Cortes and his men were horrified. Cortes told his men, "These wicked acts must stop." Cortes was right. Human sacrifice is a wicked sin.

Cortes tried to stop these wicked acts. He told Montezuma and the Aztecs about the one true God. For so long, the Aztecs knew only the false gods. They killed many people to worship their false gods. The Aztecs were amazed at

Tenochtitlan, capital of the Aztecs

what the Spanish said. Cortes told them, "The one true God does not want you to kill people. This is wrong. The true God gave His own Son Jesus. Jesus died for sin."

The Aztecs wondered, "What kind of God is this? What kind of god would give his own son to die?"

Sadly, the Aztecs did not turn from their false gods. War broke out between them and the Spanish. The Spanish did not wish to kill the Aztecs. They did want to conquer the land for Spain. They did want to teach the Aztecs about the true God. They wanted to stop all human sacrifice. But this led to a war.

The war lasted for some time. Then in 1520, Montezuma was killed in battle. Cortes and his army captured the capital city. They smashed the idols. They tore down the pagan temples. The Aztec Empire was no more. Now, Spain would rule over Mexico. Aztec gold was now sent to Spain.

Montezuma

Looking back, what should we think of Cortes? What should we think about his actions?

We should be thankful that he ended human sacrifice. We should also be thankful that some Aztecs came to know about the one true God. Some of them became Christians. But the violence was tragic. Cortes' desire for wealth and power was not good.

After Cortes, more conquistadors came. Some of them did good. But some of them did wicked things. They made the native peoples slaves. They killed many people. They committed many sins in the name of Christ.

THE CONQUEST OF PERU

To the south of the Aztecs was the vast Inca Empire. A Spanish man named Francisco Pizarro heard about the Incas. Tales of vast wealth reached his ears. Pizarro had one goal. He wanted to become rich. He gathered an army to conquer the Incas.

Francisco Pizzaro (c. 1476-1541)

Pizarro went to Peru. He traveled to the city of Cuzco. This was the capital of the Incan Empire. The Spanish captured and killed the Incan king. Then Pizarro took control of the empire.

The Spanish were far outnumbered by Incas. But the Incas followed their leader. When their king was killed, they agreed to accept this new leader from Spain. The

Incas had never seen white people before. Some thought that the Spanish were gods. They said, "The gods have come to punish us for our sins."

In Peru, Pizarro got his wish. Soon, he found more gold than he could ever have imagined. The Incan gold mines yielded tons and tons of gold. Pizarro and the king of Spain became very wealthy.

Many of the Spanish worshiped the wrong god. Many of them worshiped wealth. Jesus tells us that we cannot serve God and money. We must choose

Inca ruins in Cusco, Peru

which one we will serve. We should serve God alone.

"Do not lay up for yourselves treasures on earth, where moth and rust destroy and where thieves break in and steal; but lay up for yourselves treasures in heaven, where neither moth nor rust destroys and where thieves do not break in and steal. For where your treasure is, there your heart will be also." (Matthew 6:19-21)

The Spanish brought another weapon with them. But this weapon wasn't a sword or a spear. This was a weapon the Spanish didn't mean to bring with them. Do you know what it was? When the Spanish came to the new world, they brought diseases with them. These diseases had been in Europe for many years. But the natives in the new world had never had these diseases. Many of the natives died of smallpox and other illnesses.

BARTOLOMÉ DE LAS CASAS

More Spanish came to the new world. They started colonies. They made the natives into slaves. Some Spanish cared about the natives. But other Spanish didn't. They used these people to get rich.

Most people in Spain did not know what was going on in the new world. They didn't know all the wicked things some Spaniards were doing. But in 1542, a brave man wrote a short book. It was called *A Short Account of the Destruction of the Indies.* The author's name was Bartolomé de Las Casas. He was a Spanish priest. He lived in the new world. His home was on the island of Hispaniola. He saw firsthand many of the evils done by the Spanish. Las Casas wrote his book to tell Spain what was taking place. He wanted to stop the wicked things that were happening.

Bartolomé de Las Casas (1484-1566)

Las Casas came to the new world to teach the natives about Christ. He said, "The natives here would be blessed if they became Christians. They would be the most blessed people in all the world." But instead, many Spanish hurt or killed the natives. Las Casas called some of the Spanish "ravenous wolves." These men said they were Christians. But they did wicked things. Las Casas warned the Spanish, "The natives will never be converted if you act like this. They won't listen to us preach if we are so cruel to them."

Las Casas lamented that the natives still didn't know about God. He warned Spain that God would judge them for what they were doing. "God will judge our nation for these sins," he wrote.

OTHER SPANISH EXPLORERS

Tales of gold brought many Spanish to the new world. They searched all over the Americas for gold. In some cases, gold was right under their feet. But they didn't know it. Some gold and silver needed to be mined out of the earth.

One of these men was Francisco Vasquez de Coronado. He was inspired by the riches Pizarro found in Peru. He spent two years exploring North America. He was trying to find some cities he had heard about. These cities were called the Seven Cities of Cibola. Natives told Coronado about the cities. They told him, "The roofs of every building in these cities are made of gold!" Coronado looked everywhere for these cities. He found the Grand Canyon while he looked. He searched for two years and 7,000 miles, but he never found the golden cities.

At the same time, a Spanish man explored Florida. His name was Hernando de Soto. He also looked for a golden city. From Florida, he went north. He explored much of the American South. In 1541, he discovered the Mississippi River. But he never found the cities of gold.

These men did not find the gold they wanted so badly. But they learned much about North America. They sent word back to Europe. They told the world what they had found.

News about the Americas spread. People from England, France, and the Netherlands heard about this new world. One day, they would also send people to America.

FRANCISCO VASQUEZ DE CORONADO IN THE GRAND CANYON

Francisco Vasquez de Coronado explored modern-day New Mexico, Colorado, Kansas, and Arizona, but he never found the cities of gold.

Thatched roof cottage in Plymouth Plantation

7 WILLIAM BRADFORD AND THE PILGRIMS

He calms the storm,
So that its waves are still.
Then they are glad because they are quiet;
So He guides them to their desired haven.
Oh, that men would give thanks to the LORD for His goodness,
And for His wonderful works to the children of men! (Psalm 107:29-31)

After ten weeks at sea, the *Mayflower* had arrived. It was November 21, 1620. The men, women, and children fell to their knees. They blessed the God of heaven. They knew it was the Lord who had brought them over the large and fierce ocean. God had been merciful to them. He had carried them safely to America.

November was a difficult season to arrive in this part of the world. Winter was coming. The weather was already cold.

About 130 people had come on the ship to make this new land their home. They were eager to be on firm ground again. The *Mayflower* dropped anchor in Cape Cod Bay. Yet this was not where the ship was supposed to arrive. When it left England, it was heading to Virginia. But the ship went north instead. This happened by God's **providence**.

Providence

The Bible teaches that God governs all things that happen in the world. God is holy, wise, and good. He has a plan for His creation. God works out His holy will and plan through providence.

Winter was coming quickly. The Pilgrims could not go to Virginia now. They didn't have time before the winter set in. They decided to go ashore.

Here, on the coast of Massachusetts, the Pilgrims built a colony. They called it Plymouth Plantation.

THE PILGRIMS IN ENGLAND AND THE NETHERLANDS

Pilgrims on the *Mayflower*

The *Mayflower* left the shores of England in September 1620. The journey was not easy. Crossing the Atlantic Ocean was risky. Storms could destroy the ship. Sailors could veer off course. It took a long time to reach the new world. The ship had to cross thousands of miles of ocean to get there.

The *Mayflower* sailed at about two miles per hour. Sailors used the wind to move the ship along. When the wind blew, the ship went faster. If the wind didn't blow, it went slower. Can you imagine driving to church at two miles per hour? That's about as fast as you walk.

Over 100 people were crammed into a very small space on the ship. Many of them got seasick. Ten weeks of rocking back and forth made everyone wish for land.

God was good to the Pilgrims. He kept them safe. The Lord "guided them to their desired haven" (Psalm 107:30). That means He carried the ship where He wanted it to go.

Why did the Pilgrims leave England? If the journey was so dangerous, why did they go? Why didn't they stay at home?

The Pilgrims had a few reasons why they left England. They had trouble with the rulers there. In England, everyone in the church had to believe the same thing. They had to follow what the rulers of the land told them. The Pilgrims didn't like this. They were **Separatists**. This means they didn't want to be a part of the church like the rulers told them to. They wanted to have their own church where they could worship God. But King James wasn't happy about this. He wanted all people to worship in the way he thought was best. He persecuted the Separatists. He would not allow them to meet freely to worship God.

So the Pilgrims left England. They fled to a new country. Together, they made a new home in the Netherlands. Here, they could worship God freely. But they also needed to take care of their families. The Pilgrims got new jobs in the city of Leiden. It was not easy to make a living here. The Pilgrims had trouble in their work. But they did have freedom of worship. This was a blessing.

Modern replica of the *Mayflower*

After ten years, the Pilgrims were still having trouble in Leiden. They did not make much money. The moms and dads also began to worry about their children. They wanted their children to be godly. But the Dutch young people were not godly. They tempted the English children to do wrong things.

The Pilgrims were Christians. They wanted to live for God. They wanted to seek His kingdom. They wanted to spread the gospel across the world. Because of this, they decided to make a new home in America. In America, they would have freedom. They could worship God. But they could also bring the gospel to this new land. They could teach people about Christ.

BUILDING PLYMOUTH PLANTATION

William Bradford was a Pilgrim. He became the governor of the colony in the new world. He wrote an important book. This book tells us about the history of the Pilgrims. William explains in his book why the Pilgrims came to America. They did not come just for freedom. They also wanted to teach the natives about God. They wanted these natives to be saved from their sins. They could only be saved through faith in Jesus Christ. In his book, William wrote: "We wanted to lay a foundation. We started a colony to spread the gospel. Our work is only the beginning. It might just be a stepping stone for someone else. But maybe others will follow us."

William Bradford (1590-1657)

This is exactly what the Pilgrims did. They laid a foundation. Plymouth Plantation was one of the first colonies in America. It is part of America's Christian history.

When the Pilgrims arrived in Cape Cod Bay, winter was coming. They didn't have any houses built. They didn't know what the land was like. And they didn't know anything about the natives. They had no helpers. They only had a little food. "We will never survive this winter unless God has mercy on us," they said.

Before they went ashore, the men said, "We must form a government. We must have rules that we all agree to keep." The Pilgrims knew that all people need laws. Without laws, evildoers are not punished. That leads to more sin and trouble.

The Pilgrim men created an agreement. It was called the **Mayflower Compact**. It begins with these words: "In the Name of God, Amen." The Pilgrims put these words at the beginning because they are important words. These words showed that the Pilgrims knew God was their Ruler. He ruled over their little colony. They would follow His laws in this new land. The Compact also explained why the Pilgrims went to America. They wanted God's glory to spread across the world. They also wanted to teach others about Christ.

THE FIRST WINTER AND SPRING

And let the beauty of the LORD our God be upon us,
And establish the work of our hands for us;
Yes, establish the work of our hands. (Psalm 90:17)

The Compact was now signed. It was time to choose a spot of land for the colony. William Bradford and other men from the *Mayflower* began to explore. For six weeks, they looked for a good spot to build. At last, they chose a place. The Pilgrims began to build houses for the winter. The first winter was difficult. The Pilgrims were not ready for the cold weather. They didn't have enough food or supplies. Soon, sickness hit the colony. People ran out of food. During the first winter, half of the Pilgrims died.

But the colony survived. Spring came. The weather became warmer. Soon, it would be time to plant food. In March 1621, the Lord gave a heaven-sent gift to the colony. The Pilgrims met an Indian named Squanto. Squanto spoke English. He had been captured and taken to England. There he learned how to speak English. God was sovereign over this important meeting. Squanto introduced the Pilgrims to the leader of a nearby tribe.

Illustration of Plymouth Plantation

Squanto also showed the Pilgrims how to grow food. This new land was different than England. The Pilgrims did not know much about growing food here. Squanto taught them how to grow corn. He also showed them where to find fish. He knew all about this land. Surely, this Indian was an answer to prayer for the Pilgrims.

LIFE AT PLYMOUTH

Sing praise to the LORD, you saints of His,
And give thanks at the remembrance of His holy name. (Psalm 30:4)

The Lord blessed the colony through the summer of 1621. Now they had lived a full year in this new land. They had many reasons to be thankful to God. That fall, the Pilgrims invited the Indians to join them for a feast. Later, this feast would be called "the first thanksgiving." There was food, drink, and

Miles Standish (1584-1656)

games. The natives brought freshly killed deer. There was corn, duck, squash, beans, and barley. The Lord sustained the Pilgrims. To remember this event, Americans celebrate Thanksgiving each November.

The winter of 1621 brought new hard times. Other Indian tribes were not so friendly. One tribe sent threats to the Pilgrims. William Bradford knew they were all in danger. He and the people made defenses for the colony. They built a wall of logs to protect their homes. A military captain trained the people. His name was Miles Standish. He trained other men how to fight. He prepared them in case an attack came. This protected the colony for many years.

The first Thanksgiving at Plymouth

In 1622, Squanto died. This was heartbreaking to the Pilgrims. Squanto had become a good friend. Without him, many more colonists might have died. But the Pilgrims were glad that Squanto knew the Lord. As he was dying,

Squanto confessed faith in the true and living God.

William served as governor for many years. As a leader, he had a lot of work to do! He worked with the other colonists in the fields. He planted crops and helped to harvest them. He was also the judge. If there was a crime or dispute, William would decide who was right. He also guided the town's defenses. He took care of the colony's money too. As a governor, William was a busy man.

William died in 1657. But Plymouth Colony continued growing for many more years. It was at peace with the Indians for a long time. But in 1675, a terrible war came. Many colonists and Indians died.

After 1675, other colonies in Massachusetts grew larger than Plymouth. Plymouth stayed small. But it was still a success. It was a stepping stone for others. It led the way so other people could come to America. The Pilgrims wanted to have a city that was built for God's glory. They wanted all their lives to serve for Him. They wanted to spread the gospel. Many other colonists would seek the very same thing. God's kingdom began to grow in North America.

Marsh near Plymouth, Massachusetts

PRAYER POINTS

- **Give Thanks to God for a Christian Heritage**
  Let's thank God for giving America a Christian start. Faithful Christians like the Pilgrims brought the Christian faith to North America. They knew that Christ was their Lord and Savior. When people obey God, many blessings come. America has received many blessings from God. Let us give thanks for God's good gifts.

- **Ask God to Preserve this Christian Heritage**
  North America is changing. Many people don't believe in God. Many don't know Jesus Christ. Ask God to preserve America's Christian past. Ask the Lord to have mercy on this land.

Martha's Vineyard, Massachusetts

8 JOHN ELIOT: AMERICA'S FIRST MISSIONARY

How then shall they call on Him in whom they have not believed? And how shall they believe in Him of whom they have not heard? And how shall they hear without a preacher? (Romans 10:14)

The year was 1631. Eleven years had passed since the Pilgrims started Plymouth Plantation. The Pilgrims wanted to tell the Indians about Christ. They wanted to spread the gospel. But not very much had yet happened. Of course, the Pilgrims shared the truth with the Indians. But most of the colonists were busy with other things. They had to build houses and plant food to take care of their families.

John Eliot (1604-1690)

At first, no one was working full-time to preach to the Indians. That changed in 1631. In that year, John Eliot left England and traveled to America. He became the first full-time missionary in North America.

JOHN ELIOT SAILS FOR AMERICA

John was born in 1604. He grew up in England. The Lord gave John a gift. He could learn languages easily. John learned how to read Latin, Greek, and Hebrew. He would need this training later on in life. He would use this training to translate the Bible.

In 1631, John sailed for Boston. After he arrived, he became a pastor in Roxbury. This is not far from Boston. John would serve as a pastor and missionary for fifty-eight years. In 1632, he married a woman named Hannah.

Together, they served the Lord. God blessed them with six children. John faithfully taught his children about God.

John was a man who spent a lot of time in prayer. He spent entire days in prayer and fasting. He was also generous. He would freely give to others. Once, John received his pay from the church. The money was wrapped up in a handkerchief. As John walked home, he saw a poor family. John decided to give some money to this poor family. At first John thought, "I will give them some of my pay." John began to unwrap the handkerchief. But he couldn't get it open quickly. So he said to the family, "Here, you can have all of this." John handed the handkerchief over. It contained his entire paycheck. He knew that God would provide for him. For this reason, John freely gave to others.

God was good to John. He became a loving and faithful man. John preached God's Word faithfully. And he lovingly gave to others.

MISSIONARY TO THE INDIANS

I now send you, to open their eyes, in order to turn them from darkness to light, and from the power of Satan to God, that they may receive forgiveness of sins and an inheritance among those who are sanctified by faith in Me. (Acts 26:17-18)

Many Indian tribes lived in **New England**. For thousands of years, they didn't know about the true God. They had never seen the light of God's Word. Tribe fought against tribe. For the Indians, revenge was normal. War was common. Each tribe had witch doctors. These witch doctors would use the power of demons to harm others. The men of the tribes were lazy and wanted to be

John Eliot's home

served. Women did most of the hard work. Men thought women should do all the farming and cooking. The men fought, hunted, and relaxed. They made the women do everything else.

New England

An area in America where the first British colonies started. Today, New England includes six states in the northeastern part of the United States.

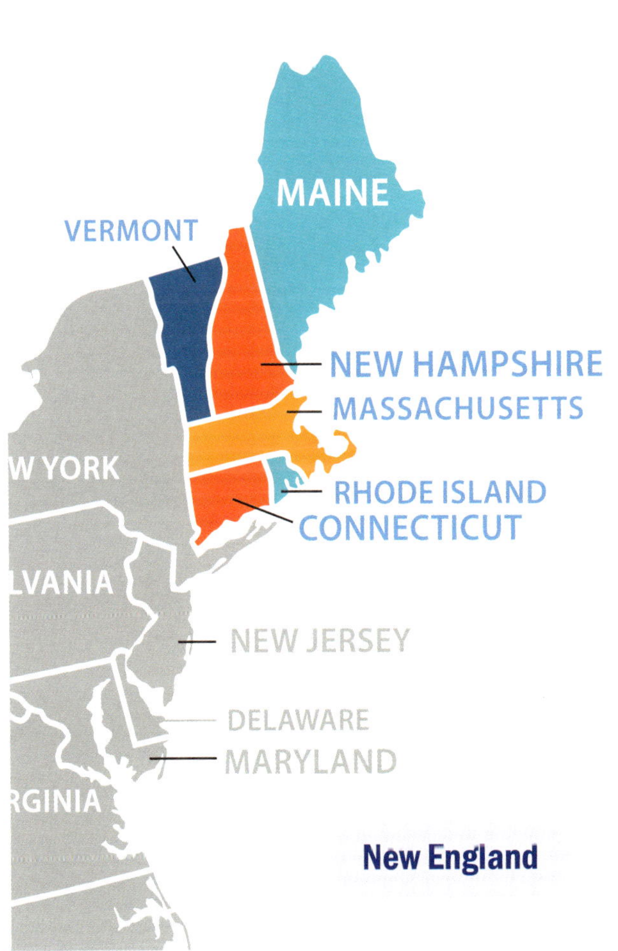

New England

This is not how our Lord Jesus taught us to live. Jesus came to be a servant to His people. He gave His life to redeem us from our sins. By looking at Jesus, we learn to serve one another as well.

Many colonists wanted the Indians to turn to God. They wanted them to stop serving their false gods. But they didn't do much to teach them God's Word. Our Lord Jesus tells us to "disciple the nations" (Matthew 28:18-20). We must teach them about God. But not many people had done this with the Indians yet.

John's heart became tender towards the Indians. He wanted God to save them. In 1643, he began studying their language. If he wanted the Indians to know Christ, then John would have to speak their language. John spent years learning the **Algonquin** language. The Indians did not write their words down. They did not have a dictionary. This made learning the language difficult. All John could do was listen to words. John listened. He wrote down the words he heard.

Algonquin is difficult to learn. Indians took many words and mashed them together. This made one very long word.

Try saying this word:

kummogkodonnattootummooetiteaongannunnarash

This word means "our question" in Algonquin. It is much easier and shorter in English. You can see why this language was hard to learn.

But John loved the Indians. He pressed on. He kept learning the language. By 1646, he was able to preach in Algonquin. He went to an Indian village. The village was called Nonantum. John prayed. Then he preached from God's Word. God opened the chief's heart. The man's name was Waban. Chief Waban began sharing the gospel with his tribe.

Later, John visited Nonantum a second time. The Indians had many questions. John answered them. They asked John, "Does God understand our prayers? Does He know what we're saying if we pray in our language?" John answered, "Of course! God understands all prayers." Another old man asked

John Eliot preaching

John, "Is it too late for me to repent?" John explained that it was not too late. The old man could still repent and be saved.

Some Indians asked, "If we don't use our witch doctors, how will we be healed from sickness?" John told them, "God can heal. Pray to Him."

These questions showed that the Holy Spirit was at work. The Indians wished to know the truth. God was working on their hearts. Soon He began to save them.

PRAYING INDIANS

When the first Indians came to Christ, people called them "praying Indians." They were called this because they prayed so much. They prayed because they wanted to. Now that they knew God, they wanted to talk to Him all the time. They were also praying for other Indians. They wanted those in their tribe and other tribes to turn from idols to the living God.

John saw many come to faith. But not all the natives liked what he said to them. Some tried to kill him. Some Indian witch doctors tried to work magic against him. But this didn't stop him. He kept preaching the Word. He would tell the Indians, "I am doing the work of God. God is with me. I do not fear your chiefs. I will keep going."

The Praying Indians were now in danger. Other natives might try to kill them. They asked John for help. They asked John, "Will you help us find a safe place to live?"

John went to the rulers of Massachusetts. He asked for land for these Praying Indians. God gave John favor with the colony. The Lord provided land for these new Christians. John helped the Praying Indians start a new

Deer in New England

town. They started this town in 1651. It was called Natick. Here, they had their own rulers to rule over them. John helped them. He taught them how to rule and govern the town.

The town of Natick was a Christian town. The Indians made a covenant for their town. It said:

We are the sons of Adam. We and our ancestors have been lost in sin for a long time. But now, God has been merciful to find us. Christ's grace will help us. We give ourselves and our children to God. We will be God's people. God will rule over us. The Lord is our judge. The Lord is our lawgiver. The Lord is our King. The Lord will save us. God's wisdom in the Bible will guide us.

The Indians of Natick really were changing. God had saved them from their sins. They began to wear clothes. The men started working. They helped the women grow food. Now they had joy in their hearts. God's praises were in their mouths. Now, when an Indian died, they did not die without hope. Now they would bury their brother or sister in hope. They had hope for the

Modern-day Natick

future. Jesus died and rose again. They knew they would rise again too.

Other towns like Natick were also started. More Indians confessed Jesus as Lord and Savior. The Lion of the tribe of Judah was on the move.

The year 1663 was a big year for John. He finished the translation of the Bible into Algonquin. This was the first Indian Bible printed in America. He also made a book of the psalms for the Indians to sing. He wrote a catechism for them as well. This would teach them the doctrine of the Bible.

By 1674, fourteen Praying Indian towns had started. There were two Indian churches as well. Altogether, there were over 1,000 Indian converts.

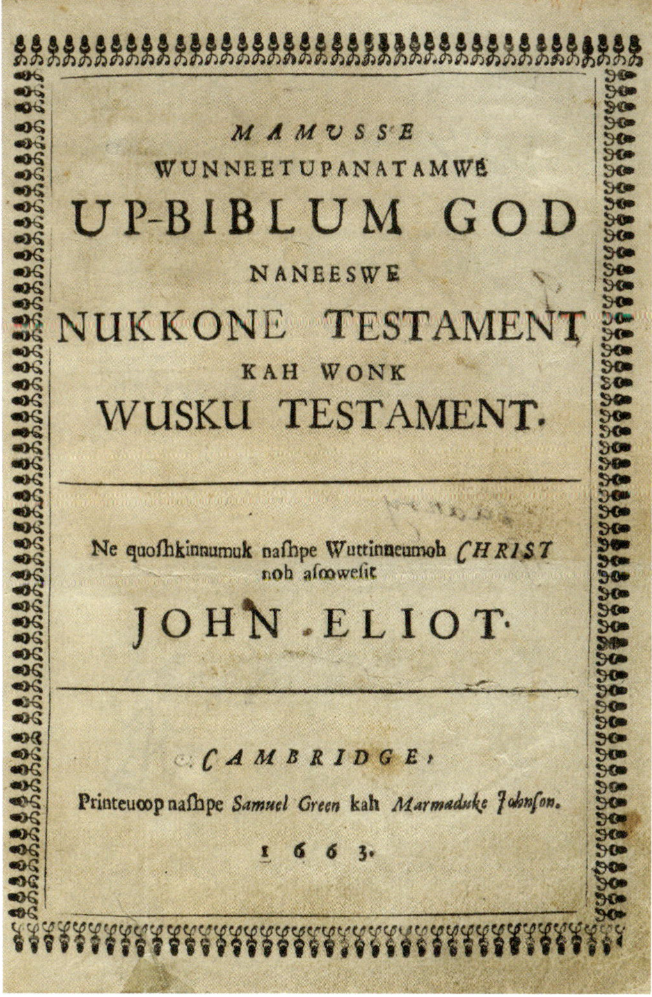

MAMUSSE
WUNNEETUPANATAMWE
UP-BIBLUM GOD
NANEESWE
NUKKONE TESTAMENT
KAH WONK
WUSKU TESTAMENT.

Ne quoſhkinnumuk naſhpe Wuttinneumoh *CHRIST*
noh aſoowesit

JOHN ELIOT.

CAMBRIDGE:
Printeuoop naſhpe *Samuel Green* kah *Marmaduke Johnſon*.
1663.

Title page of John Eliot's Bible translation

Hard times came in 1675. A war broke out between the colonists and Indians. The Indian Chief Metacomet attacked the English. The war lasted for three years. Many people died. This made some English mistrust the Praying Indians as well. John Eliot kept defending them. The war brought hardship to many. But after three years it was over. The work of the gospel went on. John kept discipling the Indians. He did not stop until his death.

On May 20, 1690, John went to be with the Lord. His last words were, "Welcome joy!" He fought the good fight. He finished the race. He kept the faith. The Lord gave him a crown of righteousness (2 Timothy 4:7-8).

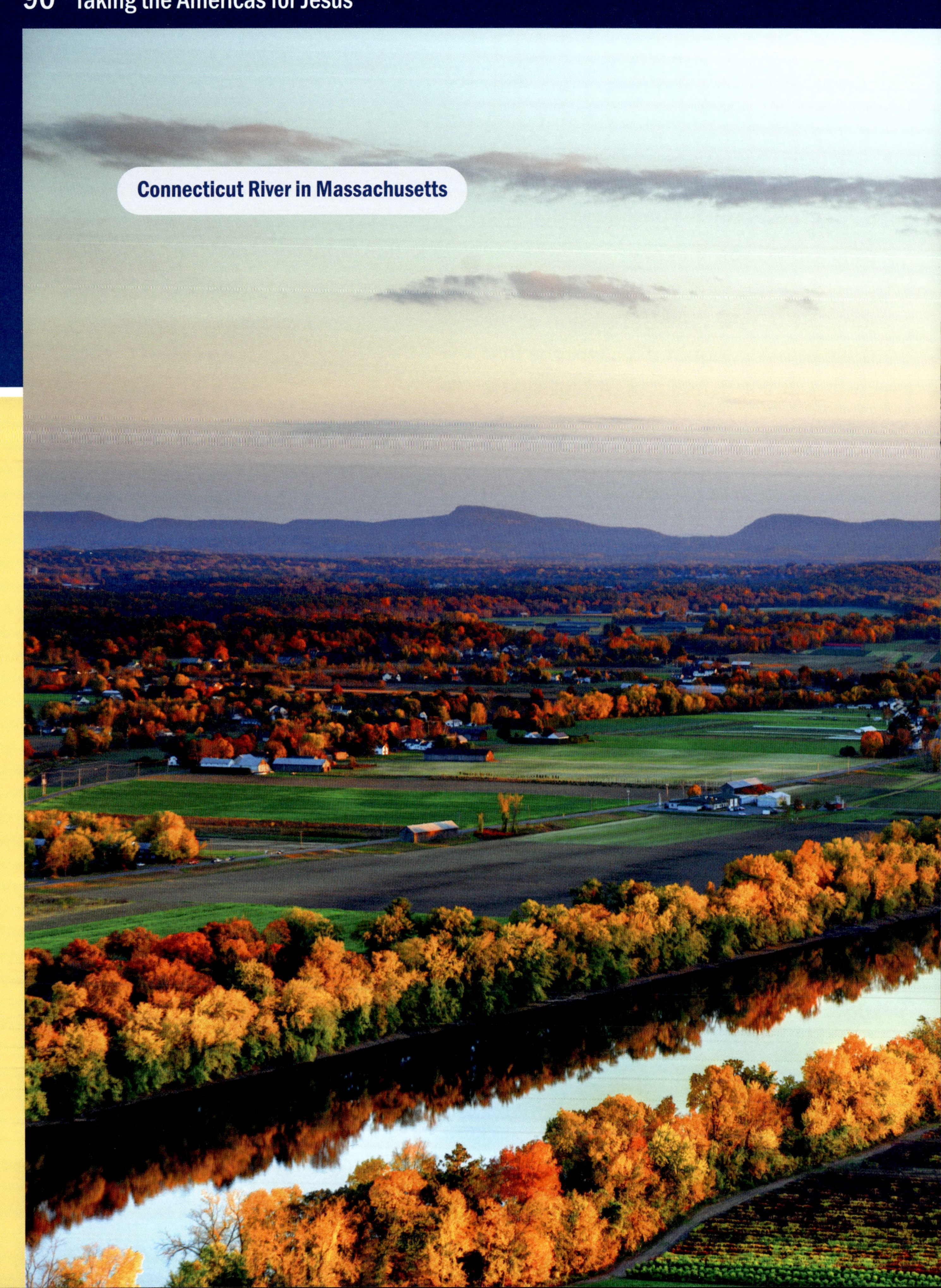

Connecticut River in Massachusetts

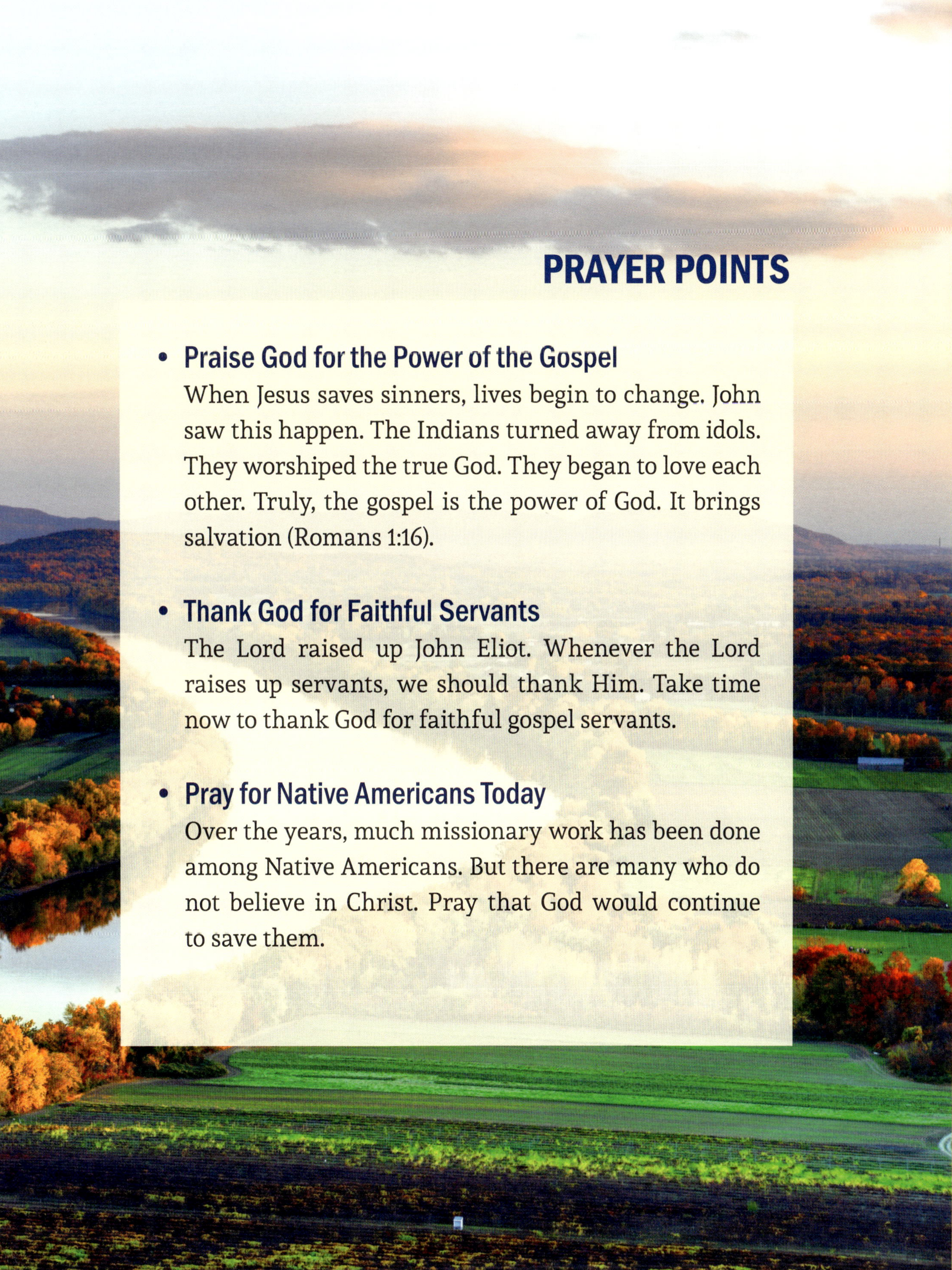

PRAYER POINTS

- **Praise God for the Power of the Gospel**
  When Jesus saves sinners, lives begin to change. John saw this happen. The Indians turned away from idols. They worshiped the true God. They began to love each other. Truly, the gospel is the power of God. It brings salvation (Romans 1:16).

- **Thank God for Faithful Servants**
  The Lord raised up John Eliot. Whenever the Lord raises up servants, we should thank Him. Take time now to thank God for faithful gospel servants.

- **Pray for Native Americans Today**
  Over the years, much missionary work has been done among Native Americans. But there are many who do not believe in Christ. Pray that God would continue to save them.

Old City of Philadelphia, Pennsylvania

9 THE GREAT AWAKENING

George Whitefield (1714-1770)

Will You not revive us again,
That Your people may rejoice in You?
Show us Your mercy, Lord,
And grant us Your salvation. (Psalm 85:6-7)

It was a cool October day in 1739. Benjamin Franklin walked the cobblestone streets of Philadelphia. He strolled toward Market Street. As he walked, he heard a loud, booming voice. Someone was preaching at the courthouse.

Benjamin saw the courthouse in the distance. Thousands were gathered. All eyes were on the courthouse steps. At the top of the steps stood a preacher. He was short and dressed in a black robe. His deep voice echoed across Market Street.

The man atop the courthouse steps was Mr. George Whitefield. He was a preacher from England.

Whitefield preached with great passion. With all his strength, he exclaimed:

In the Bible, salvation is called the free gift of God. It comes through Jesus Christ our Lord. Salvation is free. We can do nothing to earn it. God has all power. He uses this power to save sinners. No person can do anything to save himself. No man can do anything to make God show him mercy. We must believe in Jesus Christ. Through Christ, God declares us to be righteous. That is the only way we can find favor with God. God gives us this righteousness by faith. Faith is also God's gift. And this faith, if it is true faith, will show itself in love.

This was Mr. Whitefield's first visit to the city. Many people were glad to see him come. Mr. Whitefield was known all through the colonies. Wherever he went, thousands gathered to hear him preach God's Word.

Newspapers in England and America wrote about him. One paper said, "Twenty thousand gather to hear Mr. Whitefield preach!"

Benjamin Franklin (1706-1790)

Benjamin Franklin found headlines like that hard to believe. How could one man speak to so many people? How could the people hear him? This was a good question. In the 1700s, no one had microphones. They had not invented sound systems yet.

Mr. Franklin decided to run a test. How many people could hear the preacher at one time? Could Mr. Whitefield really speak to 20,000 people at once?

Benjamin began walking away from the courthouse. He walked down Market Street. Each step took him towards the river. As he walked, he got farther away from the preacher. Mr. Whitefield's voice was not as loud. But it was still crystal clear.

Then Benjamin stopped walking. Silently he did some math. After a quick math problem in his head, he stood amazed. Even so far away, he could still hear the preacher. Franklin realized that Whitefield could be heard by more than 30,000 people.

Franklin walked back to the courthouse. Mr. Whitefield kept preaching. He told the crowd about Zacchaeus the tax collector. He talked about how this man had been saved. Then he cried:

Make haste, O sinners! Make haste and come to faith in Christ. Believe in Him now. If you believe, Jesus Christ will come. He will make His eternal home in your hearts. Which of you is made willing to receive the King of glory? Which of you will obey the call like Zacchaeus did? Alas, why do you stand still? How do you know if Jesus Christ will call you again? Come then, poor, guilty sinners. Come away. Make haste, I say. Come away to Jesus Christ. The Lord invites Himself to come into the filthy houses of your souls. Do not be afraid to let Him in. He will fill you with all peace and joy. Only believe!

Benjamin Franklin did not receive Jesus that day. But he was very impressed with Mr. Whitefield. It was hard not to be impressed. This man was a powerful preacher. There was no one like him. Only he could hold thousands spellbound with his speech.

Franklin knew that Whitefield would ask for money. He was trying to raise money for an orphanage in Georgia. Benjamin thought to himself, "He won't get anything from me!"

Then Whitefield began to talk about the orphans. "The orphans in Georgia need your help! Who will give to this cause?"

Whitefield explained how much the orphans needed help. His eloquent words touched the hearts of those who heard him. Franklin dropped a few coins into the dish.

Mr. Whitefield kept speaking. Benjamin thought, "Perhaps I should give a bit more." As Whitefield ended, Franklin emptied his pocket. He gave every single coin for the orphans. As you can see, George Whitefield was a gifted preacher.

GEORGE WHITEFIELD CROSSES AMERICA

"The time is fulfilled, and the kingdom of God is at hand. Repent, and believe in the gospel." (Mark 1:15)

In the 1740s, a change came to America. God's Spirit brought revival to the land. Many people turned to the Lord. Men and women turned from their sins. Even little boys and girls ran to Christ. This time is called the **Great Awakening**.

God used preachers during this time. Through these men, God woke up the souls of men and women. He opened their hearts to believe in Christ.

George Whitefield preaching

George Whitefield was one of these preachers. Jonathan Edwards and John Wesley were others.

Whitefield began preaching in England. He traveled all over Great Britain. Sometimes he preached in church buildings. But he also preached in the open air. He preached in large meadows or on city streets. The crowds were often too large to fit into churches.

God blessed Whitefield. The Lord used his sermons to save many. Tens of thousands gathered to hear him preach. Many of those repented of their sins and believed in Jesus.

So many came to hear him that he could barely keep up. But God gave him strength. Whitefield wrote, "No church or house could contain all the people who came. I found special power given to me by God. At all times, the blessed Jesus was with me. He visited and refreshed my heart."

Whitefield wrote this in his journals:

> The crowds became bigger and bigger. On the Lord's Day, I would sometimes preach four times. The audiences were very large. Most were deeply changed by the message. For three straight months, there was no end to the people. They flocked to hear God's Word. I then preached nine times in one week.

Jonathan Edwards (1703-1758)

HOW AMERICA WAS CHANGED

> Now the Lord is the Spirit; and where the Spirit of the Lord is, there is liberty. (2 Corinthians 3:17)

John Wesley (1703-1791)

Benjamin Franklin saw people changed. He said, "I am shocked to see change taking place in the people! Before this, they didn't care about God. But now it seems like everyone is changed. Walk the streets at evening. You are sure to run into someone singing psalms."

Some didn't like Whitefield's preaching. Not everyone who heard him believed what he said. They did not want to repent. This is what happens when God's Word is preached. The Word falls on rocky ground. Some will not receive it. But the Word also falls on good soil. When it falls on good soil, the Word takes root and bears fruit.

What kind of fruit came from Mr. Whitefield's preaching? Perhaps hundreds of thousands came to saving faith in Christ. Lives were changes. Sins were repented of. The fruit of the Spirit filled many lives. Those who once

Christ Church in Philadelphia

didn't read the Bible now read it with zeal. Those who once did not pray now prayed. Those who once were drunkards found joy in God. Some who were angry were now loving. In all, Jesus Christ was magnified as a great Savior for sinners.

George Whitefield preached for many decades. He preached in England. He preached in Scotland. He preached all over the American colonies. For a time, he was the most well-known man in America.

Whitefield was not the only preacher God used. Many other faithful men also preached the gospel. During this time, God built His church in America. He made it stronger than it was before. This was a mighty work of God.

PRAYER POINTS

- **Give Thanks to God for Sending the Holy Spirit**
  The Lord poured out His Spirit on America during the Great Awakening. Many believed in the Lord. Not all came to know Him, but some did. This was God's mercy to America. Give thanks to the Lord for His saving mercy.

- **Ask God for True Revival**
  Pray that God would bless the nation you live in. Ask Him to pour out His Holy Spirit on your land. Pray that Jesus Christ would be glorified. Ask God to change hearts in your community. And ask Him to start by reviving your heart and the hearts in your family with love for God.

- **Pray for a Time to Speak about Christ**
  Pray that God would give you opportunities to share the truth about Jesus. Perhaps pray for a neighbor or friend you know. Ask God to change their hearts.

Housatonic River, Connecticut

10 DAVID BRAINERD: MISSIONARY TO THE NATIVES OF NEW ENGLAND

For I am not ashamed of the gospel of Christ, for it is the power of God to salvation for everyone who believes, for the Jew first and also for the Greek. (Romans 1:16)

David Brainerd was a missionary. He preached to the native Americans. He lived in the 1700s. He did not live long. He died when he was only twenty-nine years old. But his life changed the world. After he died, his journal was published. Many other Christians read his journal. His faith and love still encourage Christians today. Let's learn about this man of God!

David was born in 1718. He lived in Connecticut. His family was Christian. As a boy, David went to church each week. At church, he listened to long sermons. These sermons were sometimes two hours long! He also learned to sing the psalms. David learned much about God as a young man.

When David was twenty years old, his life began to change. God's Holy Spirit started to work in him. David knew he was a sinner. He knew that he needed Jesus to save him. When God saved him, he was filled with joy. He wanted to preach God's Word. He wanted to see other people trust in Jesus Christ.

In 1739, David went to Yale College. He was then trained by a pastor. The pastor's name was Jedidiah Mills. Pastor Mills taught David more about the Bible. David loved the Lord Jesus more and more. He followed Christ. He also wanted to see other people believe in Jesus. He began to pray for the souls of the natives. Most Indians in America did not worship the true God. They worshiped things in God's world instead. This is idolatry. David was sad about the Indians. Would they go to heaven or hell? He knew they would be lost without Christ. He wanted to do something to help them. He wanted to tell them about the Savior.

Yale College

In 1742, David began preaching. He went to the Indians to teach them about Jesus. One other pastor went with him. They began telling the natives about God's Word. They first went to an Indian village on the **Housatonic River**. This river is in the state of Connecticut.

The Lord blessed David's preaching. The natives cried out for God's mercy. God showed them that they were full of sin. Some of the natives put their trust in Jesus. This was the first time David preached to the Indians. In just one year, he preached sixty sermons. He traveled all over the colonies of America.

Next, David decided to go west. There were more Indians in the west. They needed the Savior too. He went to a place called Stockbridge. The Mohican Indians lived there. Wherever David went, he preached the same message.

David said this about his preaching: "I taught that men are sinners. All sinners will be judged by God. Then I told them that Christ could save them. Christ was a great Savior. All who believe in Jesus will be saved."

David loved the Indians. That is why he preached to them. But some people didn't love them. English and Dutch settlers tried to stop David. These

David Brainerd ministering to indians

men wanted land. They treated the Indians like enemies. They didn't want anyone to do good to the natives. This was why they tried to stop David.

But David didn't stop preaching. He kept sharing the good news with the natives.

In June 1743, David went even farther west than Stockbridge. He found another group of natives. While he was with them, he lived in a **wigwam**. Then he spent every day teaching the Bible to the natives. This was hard work. David often struggled to have food. Some days he did not eat at all. He sacrificed much for Jesus Christ.

Wigwam

A kind of tent used by native Americans. A wigwam was built using bark, animal hides, or reeds. It is similar to a teepee.

In 1744, David went down the Delaware River. He found some Indians tribes there. They had not heard about Jesus. David wanted to teach them. But

Example of Native American Wigwam

then he became sick. He had a disease called **tuberculosis**. This disease made it hard for him to breathe. For a few weeks, David lay in bed. He couldn't get up. But that summer, he began to get better. He started traveling and preaching more.

Lapowinsa, chief of the Delaware Indians

The settlers kept trying to stop David. Many natives also tried to stop him. Indian witch doctors tried to scare him. They tried to poison him by using their evil magic. David was not afraid of them. He challenged the witch doctors. He said, "Why can't your magic harm me?" He knew the answer. The witch doctors knew too. God was protecting David. Those witch doctors could not win against God's power.

Sometimes, the Indians trusted in Jesus. But many did not want to leave their idols. Many of the Indian men wanted to hunt. They were too busy to care about God. They did not want to listen to Bible teaching. This made work very hard for David. He loved the Indians. But it was harder to love them when they didn't want to hear about God. David asked God to give him more compassion. He wanted to love the natives even more.

Satan blinded the eyes of many Indians. This is what the Bible says:

> The god of this world has blinded the minds of those who don't believe. They can't see the light of the good news of Christ's glory. He is the likeness of God. (2 Corinthians 4:4 NIRV)

God is the only One who can break through hard hearts. David Brainerd knew this. He prayed and fasted. He asked God to break through these barriers. The Lord did mighty things. He saved some of the Indians. But many still rejected Christ. David was grieved by this. He even wondered whether he should stop preaching. But God had more work for him to do.

Stokes State Forest, New Jersey

David traveled to a new place in June 1745. He was discouraged. But he decided to keep going. That month, he went to an Indian tribe in New Jersey.

At first, he preached to small crowds. Only twenty or thirty people came to hear him. But these Indians began to mourn over their sins. They invited their friends to hear David. One native woman told David she wanted to change. She said, "I wish God would change my heart."

More and more Indians came to hear about Jesus. Then, in August 1745, something amazing happened. Over 100 Indians came to faith. David preached. The Indians cried out to God, "Have mercy on me! Have mercy on me!" Jesus saved them. Then their lives began to change. David baptized many of them. These Indians were "new creations in Christ" (2 Corinthians 5:17). Their way of life changed. Now they loved God. Now they prayed to Him all the time. Many of them became preachers to other Indians. Praise God!

In August 1746, David made his last trip into Indian lands. He was still sick. Yet he still didn't give up. But by March of 1747, he was too sick to travel. He stayed in the home of Jonathan Edwards. This man was the pastor of a church in Massachusetts. David hoped to get better. But God was calling him home to be with Jesus. He went to be with the Lord. The date was October 9, 1747. David died when he was only twenty-nine years old.

Jonathan Edwards read David's diary. He said, "We should make this into a book so other people can read it." When David wrote his diary, he didn't know that God would use his writing. But God has used this book to help many people. David's love, humility, and passion still inspire those who read his diary. David gave up everything to serve Jesus. He also loved lost souls.

Squantz Pond, Connecticut

11 JONATHAN EDWARDS: A LOVE FOR GOD'S GLORY

The heavens declare the glory of God;
And the firmament shows His handiwork. (Psalm 19:1)

It was a warm summer afternoon in Connecticut. Thirteen-year-old Jonathan Edwards sat under a tree. He watched as a spider jumped from one branch to another. The spider was called a flying spider, though it had no wings.

The spider moved perfectly from branch to branch. Not once did it fall. Not once did it get hurt as it launched its small body into the air.

Jonathan held a notepad in his hand. As he watched, he sketched the spider's jumps on his notepad. This tiny creature filled the boy's heart with wonder. Jonathan thought to himself, "God's world is wonderful. Every part of His creation is stunning. He made this spider to move with such skill. Not only is the spider able to jump perfectly. But it seems like the spider is having fun at the same time!"

Jonathan learned many things about God that day. He saw God's wisdom as he watched the spider. He also saw God's beauty and glory in that little bug.

From the time when he was a little boy, Jonathan loved the outdoors. He loved to take walks in God's creation. He saw God's glory in the rivers, the grass, the flowers, and animals. He loved God's glory.

As he grew older, he also saw God's glory in the Bible. Each Lord's Day, he went to church with his family. His father was the pastor of the church. Jonathan's grandfather Solomon was also a pastor. He preached in the nearby village of Northampton.

Even as a child, Jonathan learned about God. Each week, he heard the Bible preached and read. This was a blessing from God. Many children in the world don't grow up with Christian parents. Many children don't have Bibles.

Yale College, New Haven

At age thirteen, Jonathan went to Yale College. He studied many things. He loved God's world, so he wanted to become a scientist. To study God's works was a joy to him. However, he would not become a scientist. The Lord had other plans for him.

LIVING FOR THE LORD

One day, Jonathan was reading the Bible. He was now seventeen years old. He turned to Paul's first letter to Timothy. He began reading. Soon he came to this verse:

> Now to the King eternal, immortal, invisible, to God who alone is wise, be honor and glory forever and ever. Amen. (1 Timothy 1:17)

The Spirit of God moved upon the young man's heart. Jonathan wrote, "As I read these words, there came into my soul a sense of God's amazing glory. From then on, I was thinking often about God. I saw the glory of Jesus Christ. I knew the glory of His salvation."

Jonathan Edwards (1703-1758)

Jonathan wanted to preach. He wanted to tell other people about the glory of God. He wanted to proclaim the good news of the Lord Jesus. After he finished at Yale, he decided to become a pastor.

In 1722, he moved to New York City. He preached God's Word at a church on Wall Street. He was only nineteen years old.

While in New York, God's Spirit was teaching Jonathan. He became sad as he thought about his past sins. He said to himself, "How wicked I was before I believed in Jesus!" He often cried. He was grieved by his own sins.

Jonathan wanted to follow the Lord with his whole heart. He made up his mind to work on this. So he wrote a list of **resolutions**. A resolution is when you decide to do something and say you will do it. Jonathan wrote his resolutions down. He wrote seventy of them.

The Bible says, "exercise yourself toward godliness" (1 Timothy 4:7). This means we should work hard to be godly. Jonathan made up his mind to do this. He wanted to follow the Lord.

Here are some of his resolutions:

I know that I can't do anything without God's help. I pray that God will help me to keep these resolutions. For the sake of Christ.

Resolved that I will do whatever is most to God's glory. Resolved to do that which is good. Resolved to do this no matter how hard it may be.

Jonathan made many resolutions. He was not perfect in keeping them. But they were good reminders for him.

> I resolve to never lose any time. I resolve to use time in the most profitable way I can.
>
> I resolve to study the Scriptures every day.
>
> I resolve to find ways to love others and serve others.

PASTOR IN NORTHAMPTON

In 1727, Jonathan moved to the town of Northampton. He served as a pastor with his grandfather, Solomon Stoddard.

Pastor Solomon was getting older. He was eighty-three years old. Jonathan was a young man. After Pastor Solomon went to be with the Lord, Jonathan would be the next pastor.

The Lord was also kind to Jonathan by giving him a wife. Jonathan married his wife Sarah that year. Together they would have eleven children.

Illustration of Northampton

In 1729, Pastor Solomon went to be with the Lord. Jonathan was now the only pastor in his church. He loved to preach God's Word. The people loved his preaching too.

Jonathan prayed often. He asked God to show His power to His people. He wanted to see every person in the town saved from their sins. In time, God began to answer his prayers. In 1734, the Holy Spirit saved many people.

Jonathan wrote what happened:

Almost every person in the town is concerned about eternal things. Many in town did not care about the Lord. But now almost everyone is concerned about their soul. Many put their trust in Jesus Christ. The young people in town now spend their time talking about Jesus. They speak often about how Jesus died for them.

This move of God took place in Northampton. But God wasn't finished yet. Soon, all across the colonies, people began to turn to God.

This time in history is called the **Great Awakening**.

One day, Jonathan went to the town of Enfield. He preached a sermon called "Sinners in the Hands of an Angry God." It was a sermon that talked about God's judgment. It also talked about Jesus and how He saves. In the sermon, Jonathan warned his hearers about their sins. He told them that the judgment of God was coming.

While he preached, people began to cry out to God. Many shouted, "Lord, save me!" It was hard to hear the sermon because so many people were crying out. Jonathan asked the people to be quiet. "Please, allow me to continue," he asked. Then he kept preaching.

"If you are not in Christ, be warned. God's wrath is hanging over you. You must flee to Jesus. In Jesus, you will be saved!"

God used this sermon in a powerful way. Many people repented of their sins. They put their faith in Christ. By God's mercy, many men, women, and children were saved.

Edwards in Stockbridge, Massachussetts

MISSIONARY TO THE INDIANS

Jonathan served as a pastor for twenty years. In 1751, the Lord called him to a new work. To the west of Northampton stood the small town of Stockbridge. Jonathan and his family packed all their belongings on wagons. Then they made the forty-mile journey to Stockbridge.

It was a small town. It sat on the edge of the frontier. Stockbridge was made up of seventeen houses and a church. The Housatonic River flowed nearby.

Edwards on Stockbridge, Massachusetts

For six years, Jonathan preached to the Mohican and Mohawk tribes. Preaching to the Indians was different than preaching at his old church. Jonathan made his sermons shorter. He used simple words. The Indians didn't know much about God or the Bible. Jonathan had to talk in a simple way to the Indians.

Jonathan told them, "We invite you to come and enjoy the light of God's Word. It is ten thousand times brighter than the sun. It is like a sweet and beautiful flower in spring. Receive God's Word in your hearts. Then you will be prepared to live in heaven. Heaven is a world of light. There you will shine forth forever. You will live in Christ's kingdom forever."

Jonathan gave the Indians the best news ever. He gave them the news about Jesus.

FINAL DAYS IN PRINCETON

In 1758, some men asked Jonathan to come to Princeton College. They wanted him to be the president of this college. Jonathan was a good writer. He was a good teacher too. Princeton wanted him to lead the college. Jonathan agreed. He moved to Princeton.

But he did not live long in Princeton. An outbreak of smallpox came to the college. Smallpox was a dangerous disease. It was common in America at that time.

Jonathan received a vaccine for smallpox. He hoped the vaccine would protect him from the disease. But it didn't. Instead, it made him very ill.

Jonathan died on March 22, 1758. He was fifty-four years old. His wife Sarah was heartbroken. Her dear husband was no longer with her. Sarah was sad. But she still believed in God. She wrote, "My God lives! He has my heart."

Let us praise God for faithful pastors like Jonathan Edwards. The Lord is full of mercy. He shows this mercy to the world when He sends preachers to it. Through men like Edwards, men and women come to know Jesus Christ. They begin to love and serve Him as their Lord and Savior.

Modern-day Stockbridge

Oneida Lake, New York

SAMUEL KIRKLAND: PEACEMAKER TO THE INDIANS

12

Pursue peace with all people, and holiness, without which no one will see the Lord. (Hebrews 12:14)

Its blue waters stretch twenty-one miles long by five miles wide. Oneida Lake is the largest lake in New York. It is a place of great beauty. But it is not only beautiful. It is also an important part of history. Near this lake, the Oneida people lived. They were a tribe of Indians.

The Oneida tribe didn't know God. But He showed mercy to them. He sent a preacher of the gospel to them. That preacher's name was Samuel Kirkland. From 1765 to 1808, Samuel served the Indians of New York.

Samuel Kirkland (1741-1808)

The Indians and the American colonists often fought with each other. They fought over land. They fought each other for crops and animals. They often lacked love for each other. This was not pleasing to God.

By God's grace, Samuel was a loving man. Because Samuel showed love to the Indians, they began to love him too. The Lord blessed his efforts. He became a beloved friend of the Oneida Indians.

"Blessed are the peacemakers," our Lord Jesus said (Matthew 5:9). Samuel Kirkland knew this verse well. He put it into practice many times. Samuel was a man of peace.

SAMUEL'S MINISTRY BEGINS

The Lord gave Samuel a special love for the Indians. Many colonists did not care about the natives. But Samuel did. After college, he set out to reach the Indians.

Living among the Indians could be dangerous. Would Samuel lose his life? He did not know. However, he was strong in faith. He wrote, "God is almighty. God is everywhere. God can protect me among the Indians just like anywhere else. Jesus Christ is with me. He can protect me as I share the good news of His gospel."

Seneca Chief

For eighteen months, Samuel lived among the Seneca Indians. It was not easy. At times, he suffered from severe hunger. The natives often threatened to kill him. But he kept going. It was love for Christ and love for the natives that kept him going.

Samuel was adopted into the chief's home. Over time, he learned their language. Through his faithfulness, the Lord blessed his work. Some of the Senecas put their trust in Jesus.

After working with the Senecas, Samuel moved to be with the Oneida tribe. He served the Oneidas for about forty years. In 1767, he wrote some good news about his work.

I rejoice! God has blessed this place in many ways. We can see here a glorious work of God's grace. A few months ago, this was a cruel place. God was not worshiped. The Oneidas worshiped false gods. But now, many of them are Christian. Now, in their huts, the true God is worshiped. Now they are joyful!

Samuel lived alone with the Indians for four years. Then, in 1769, God blessed Samuel with a wife. Her name was Jerusha Bingham. Now Samuel had a family. He needed to expand his home. His little log cabin was not big enough. It was only ten feet long and ten feet wide. Samuel made the house bigger. Now it was twenty feet long and sixteen feet wide.

The Oneida mission kept growing. Samuel helped build a church. A sawmill was constructed. A blacksmith shop was opened. Samuel taught the gospel. The Indians learned new skills. They learned how to farm the

Samuel Kirkland among the Oneida

land. They planted their fields with grain. Instead of war and bloodshed, God blessed them with His peace.

AMERICAN WAR FOR INDEPENDENCE

Love bears all things, believes all things, hopes all things, endures all things. (1 Corinthians 13:7)

Trouble came to Samuel's work in 1775. On April 19, the American War for Independence began. The colonists went to war against the British. This war lasted for many years. It didn't end until 1783.

Samuel loved his country. He believed the colo-

George Washington (1732 - 1799)

nies were right to fight for freedom. He became a pastor to many of the American soldiers. At the same time, he also worked with the Indians.

George Washington was the general of the Continental Army. He was glad for what Samuel was doing. He asked Samuel to help keep peace between the natives. The British tried to get the Indians to fight against the colonists. Some Indians joined the British. Others helped the colonists. Samuel often helped to bring peace when trouble started.

The Oneida people loved Samuel. When the British tried to drive Samuel away, the natives would not allow it. The tribal leaders wrote this to the British:

> We love our pastor. He is a peaceful man. He does not harm anyone. He works hard to teach us God's Word. He acts like a true servant of Jesus. For this reason, we love our pastor. We do not want him to leave. We will not part with him. We ask you to stop trying to drive him away.

In 1783, the war ended. The American colonies were free. People across the nation began to rejoice.

Surrender of the British at Yorktown, 1781

Samuel was glad the war was over. Now he could spend his life serving the natives. He kept preaching God's Word to the Indians.

SPIRITUAL HARVEST

Now the Lord is the Spirit; and where the Spirit of the Lord is, there is liberty. (2 Corinthians 3:17)

The years 1785 and 1786 were filled with rejoicing. The Lord saved many Oneida. They were hungry for God's Word. So many wanted to hear Samuel preach that there was not enough room for them all. Natives who got saved wanted to learn more about God. Samuel stayed up all night with some of them. He answered all their questions.

Samuel was a generous man. He gave almost all his money to feed and care for the Indians. In one week, he fed almost 100 people. This was hard work. But it was worth it. He was filled with joy when he saw the natives believe in God.

Each spring, new life starts to grow. Little plants begin to grow, and flowers start to bud. That was true in a spiritual way in the spring of 1786. That spring, a seventy-year-old Indian was saved. He held a seat on the Indian council. He had lived in sin for almost fifty years. Now he turned to the Lord. He asked Samuel to baptize him. The natives were amazed when this old man came to Christ. Other Indians turned to the Lord as well.

Samuel knew that the Holy Spirit was working in these people. He wrote:

I believe this is God's work of grace. It is easy to see the changes in the natives' lives. It has been seven months since anyone got drunk. Some Indians who were very wicked are now different. Instead of their old evil ways, these same Indians are now praying. Instead of being lazy, they are now working hard.

One morning, Samuel walked through the Indian village. His heart was

Oneida Lake at sunrise

filled with joy. As he walked, he praised God. What he saw was truly amazing. "I walked around the village around 10 AM. I was filled with joy to hear family devotions. The Oneida were singing God's praises. Families were crying out to God in prayer."

What God did through Samuel is truly amazing. God's Spirit filled him and the Indians with love for each other.

Samuel kept on loving the Indians until he died in 1808. Through him, the Lord God blessed the Oneida. He saved many from this tribe. Because of Samuel, many of these natives are praising God today.

Pinware River, Labrador, Canada

13 THE ESKIMOS OF LABRADOR

Modern-day Herrnhut

I will praise You, O Lord, among the peoples;
I will sing to You among the nations.
For Your mercy reaches unto the heavens,
And Your truth unto the clouds. (Psalm 57:9-10)

"My dear Jens, have you heard of the Eskimos?" Nikolaus asked. "They live in Labrador. They seem to be a violent and savage people! Why, they killed our dear brother John Erhardt!"

Brother John had gone as a missionary to Labrador. His mission did not last long. Soon after he arrived, the Eskimos killed him.

Jens answered, "Yes, I've heard of the Eskimos. They are wicked. But if Jesus saves them from their sins, they will be different. They will be new creations in Christ. Someday, I would like to go to Labrador. I want to teach them about Christ."

Nikolaus Zinzendorf

Jens Haven was a short man from Denmark. His friends called him "Little Jens." He lived in a town called Herrnhut (pronounced "hern-hoot"). He was part of a group of Christians called **Moravians**. They had this name because many of them came from Moravia.

Nikolaus Zinzendorf was a leader in Herrnhut. He told Jens, "If you want to be a missionary to the Eskimos, you must first learn their language. Go to Greenland. Learn the language. Then perhaps you can go to the Eskimos."

That is what Jens did. For four years (1758-1762), he lived in Greenland. He learned the Eskimos' language.

In 1764, the Lord opened the way for Jens to go to Labrador in Canada. Jens traveled with the British. At that time, Labrador was under British control.

On September 4, he met the Eskimos of Labrador for the first time.

JENS BEFRIENDS THE ESKIMOS

He has shown you, O man, what is good;
And what does the Lord require of you
But to do justly,
To love mercy,
And to walk humbly with your God? (Micah 6:8)

One day, Jens rowed his little fishing boat into the harbor. He drew near to a group of Eskimos and shouted to them.

"Come over to me. I have something to say to you. I am your friend."

Jens was dressed like an Eskimo. He was also short like the Eskimos.

An Eskimo replied, "You must be one of us!"

Jens then said, "I am here to be your friend."

Eskimo family

For the next two days, Jens stayed with the Eskimos. He took out a letter of safe conduct given to him by the British.

He stood up and read from the letter.

"My friends, I am here to tell you that Labrador is now a colony of Britain. The king of that land, George III, has sent me to you. He sent me here to preach the gospel. I ask you to promise to do good and not murder anymore. I will come again next year. I want to tell you more about Jesus who died for the sins of the world."

The Eskimos received Jens with joy. It seemed that the Eskimos wanted a missionary. Jens returned to Europe and told the Moravians what happened. "Brothers, it is time to start a mission among the Eskimos. Let us return to Labrador!"

MISSION STATIONS IN LABRADOR

Be still, and know that I am God;
I will be exalted among the nations,
I will be exalted in the earth! (Psalm 46:10)

The next year, the Moravians returned to Labrador. This time, four men went. Jens and one of the other men stayed in the Eskimo camp.

The Eskimos said to them, "You are not like the other men from Europe. You do not come with guns."

The Eskimos saw that these men were different. The missionaries

Eskimos of Labrador

wanted to do them good. They told the Eskimos, "We would like to purchase land from you."

The Eskimos agreed. Jens and his friend paid a fair price for the land. They did not steal land from the Eskimos. They showed respect to them. This was helpful for building a relationship.

The Moravians now built mission stations in Labrador. Eleven men and three women came to live in Labrador. There were two preachers, a doctor, cooks, and builders. They made a good team. Doctors cared for the sick. Builders built houses. Preachers taught the people about Christ. The women cooked and sewed. They also became friends with the Eskimo women. The Eskimo women learned to trust these women from Europe.

Each summer, when the ice was gone, a ship came from London. It brought supplies for the mission station. The men at the station sent supplies from Labrador back to London. Seal skins, fox skins, cod-liver oil, and more was sent to London.

Good things happened. The Eskimos learned to live better. They stopped killing and stealing. The missionaries were thankful for this. But this did not mean the Eskimos had been saved. Only Jesus can save us from sin. We cannot save ourselves.

For almost thirty years, only a few Eskimos turned to Jesus Christ. The Moravians kept praying.

EXPOSING DARKNESS

The god of this world has blinded the minds of those who don't believe. They can't see the light of the good news of Christ's glory. He is the likeness of God. (2 Corinthians 4:4 NIRV)

In time, the Moravians learned about the false god the Eskimos worshiped. One of the Eskimos was a man named Tuglavina. He claimed to have power from his false god Torngak. This man acted like a king over the Eskimos. He said his false god would tell him who should live and die. Tuglavina used evil powers to hurt his fellow Eskimos.

The Eskimos feared Tuglavina. Perhaps he would hurt them if they became Christians. This was a big reason why the Eskimos would not come to Christ.

Tuglavina said to the Eskimos, "Our great Torngak controls the wind and waves. It is he who provides food for us. If you serve him, he will provide seals and foxes for you."

Jens Haven told the Eskimos, "Torngak is a false god. There is only one true God. There is only one Savior. His name is Jesus Christ. Repent of your sins. Believe in Christ. Then you will be saved! The one true God is the only One who gives life and food."

Then, in 1793, God changed Tuglavina's heart. He became a Christian. He repented of his wickedness. He was now a humble man. He even joined the Moravians and told others about Jesus.

After Tuglavina turned to the Lord, other Eskimos also believed.

The winds of God's grace blew strongly in 1804. The Spirit of God visited this people. Many repented of their sins. The Eskimos were now turning to the Lord!

One man named Siksigak visited the mission house. The Moravians opened the door. Siksigak fell down at their feet. He cried out, "I am a sinner.

I am lost. I am going to hell."

"Repent and believe in Jesus, Siksigak. You will be saved. Turn from your wicked ways. God is merciful."

Siksigak turned to God. Now he was a new man. Before, he had been angry with his wife. But now he loved her again. Later, he became a powerful preacher.

At a church service in one mission station, an Eskimo woman stood up. "I have been the most wicked woman in this land." She put her trust in the Lord Jesus. The Moravians were astounded. God's Spirit was filling the land.

The Eskimos turned away from sin and worshiped the Lord. Thirty years of hard work was worth it. God blessed the Moravian mission. Thanks be to God for His mercy to the Eskimos of Labrador!

Moravian church in Labrador

Canadian Moose

And let us not grow weary while doing good, for in due season we shall reap if we do not lose heart. (Galatians 6:9)

Tyringham, Massachusetts

LEMUEL HAYNES: PASTOR IN NEW ENGLAND

It was a dark night in Granville, Massachusetts. A fire crackled in the fireplace of the small cottage. Next to the chimney sat a young boy. Eight-year-old Lemuel sat crouched in the chimney corner. He was reading the Bible. Slowly, he sounded out the words of Romans 1, verse 16:

> For I am not . . . ashamed of the gospel of Christ . . . for it is the power of God . . . to salvation for everyone who believes.

Lemuel was learning how to read. Next to him sat his spelling book and hymn book. Day after day, night after night, he kept reading.

In time, Lemuel read the entire Bible. He memorized many passages from it. His diligent study of God's Word would pay off. One day, he would become a pastor.

GROWING UP

> When my father and my mother forsake me,
> Then the LORD will take care of me. (Psalm 27:10)

Lemuel was born in 1753. He lived in the home of the Rose family. His birth parents left him when he was just five months old. Lemuel was an orphan. A deacon by the name of David Rose took him home and took care of him. Lemuel was an indentured servant. He would serve in the Rose family until he turned twenty-one.

Indentured Servant

A person who served someone for a period of time. Most black people in America were slaves permanently. They would only become free if they could buy their freedom. Indentured servants were not permanent slaves. They were free after they served the agreed-upon time.

Lemuel's father was a black man. His mother had white skin. Lemuel's skin was also black. At this time in America, most black people were slaves. For a boy like Lemuel, the color of his skin could make life difficult. Sometimes, other children called him mean names.

Being an orphan was difficult. Yet God was merciful to Lemuel.

The Lord blessed Lemuel with the Rose family. Deacon David Rose and his wife loved the Lord. They faithfully taught Lemuel the Bible. Lemuel said this about the Rose family: "David Rose was a godly man. His wife loved me very much. She treated me like I was her own child."

Lemuel Haynes (1753 - 1833)

Because Lemuel was a servant, he did not go to school. But he taught himself. He read many books. Most importantly, he read the Bible.

In the Bible, Lemuel read about the Lord Jesus. He learned that Jesus came into the world to save sinners like him. Lemuel confessed his sins. He prayed that God would save him.

As Lemuel grew older, he loved the Bible more and more. He thought to himself, "Maybe God has called me to be a pastor."

Fort Ticonderoga, where Lemuel Haynes served for a time

LEMUEL BECOMES A PASTOR

How beautiful upon the mountains
Are the feet of him who brings good news,
Who proclaims peace,
Who brings glad tidings of good things,
Who proclaims salvation. (Isaiah 52:7)

Every Saturday night, the Rose family sat down for family worship. During this time, they got ready for Sunday, the Lord's Day. They would read a printed sermon and pray. This helped them prepare for worship the next day. Mr. Rose asked Lemuel to lead the family one night.

"Lemuel, would you read us the sermon you chose?"

"Yes. The sermon is based on John 3:3."

Lemuel read the verse: "Jesus answered and said to him, 'Truly, I say to you, unless a man is born again, he is not able to see the kingdom of God.'"

Then Lemuel began to explain the Bible verse.

"This work of saving is too great for men or angels to do. Only God can change the human heart. God's Holy Spirit works in the heart of man. The Holy Spirit causes a person to be born again."

Lemuel went on and finished the sermon. The Rose family was impressed by what they heard.

Mr. Rose asked, "Lemuel, whose sermon did you read? That was very good!"

Lemuel replied, "I wrote it, Mr. Rose."

The Rose family was amazed. Young Lemuel had studied the Bible verse and written the sermon. Clearly, God had given him a gift for Bible teaching.

Mr. Rose promised to help Lemuel study to become a pastor.

In 1775, Mr. Rose's plans were stopped. In this year, the American colonies went to war with the British. Lemuel served as a soldier for a short time. But in October 1776, he became ill and was sent home.

That was the end of Lemuel's service. But he was still devoted to the American cause. He loved freedom. He wanted the American colonies to be free from Britain.

In 1779, Lemuel started to study with two pastors. Pastor Daniel and Pastor William trained him. The next year, Lemuel became a preacher. He began to preach in churches throughout New England.

God blessed Lemuel with a wife in 1783. Her name was Elizabeth Babbit. Together, they had ten children.

1785 is a special year in American history. In that year, Lemuel Haynes became the first ordained black pastor in America. He became a pastor in Vermont and served there for thirty years.

Lemuel learned that life as a pastor could be very difficult. His church was small. Most of the members were older. There were only a few young people in the church. Lemuel prayed to God for spiritual awakening. He asked the Lord to add more people to the church.

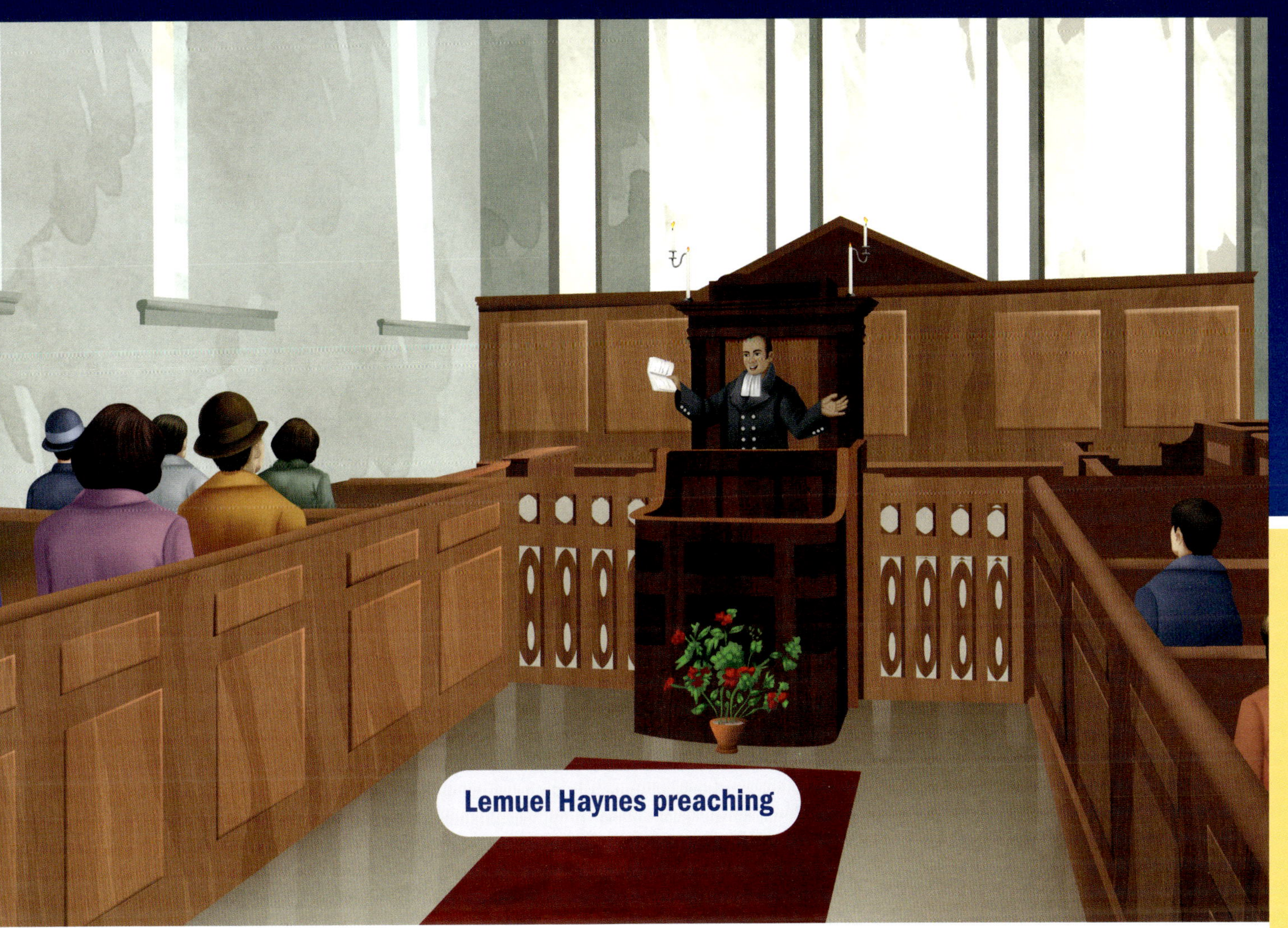

Lemuel Haynes preaching

Here and there, church members were moved by God's Word. But after fifteen years, a great work of God appeared. It began one night when a young man visited Pastor Lemuel.

"Pastor, I've been convicted of my sins. I've been foolish. I have broken God's commandments. How can I be saved?"

Soon, more of the young people were coming to Pastor Lemuel. They turned from their sins. Children wanted to pray more and read God's Word. Some enemies of Christ in the town also were converted. In 1808, over one hundred people joined the church. God answered Lemuel's prayers!

LEMUEL WRITES AGAINST SLAVERY

Growing up as a black child, Lemuel thought often about other black people in America. He wanted slavery to end. He wrote a book called *Liberty Further Extended*. In this book, Lemuel said, "Liberty is a jewel. It is a gift from God."

Lemuel argued that freedom was a blessing. This is what the Bible teaches in 1 Corinthians 7.

Were you a slave when God chose you? Don't let it trouble you. But if you can get your master to set you free, do it. Those who were slaves when the Lord chose them are now the Lord's free people. Those who were free when God chose them are now slaves of Christ. (1 Corinthians 7:21-22 NIRV)

Lemuel taught others that the gospel made peace between white and black people. In Jesus, all people are part of the same family. They are part of God's family. Paul taught this in the Bible.

For He Himself is our peace, who has made both one, and has broken down the middle wall of separation, having abolished in His flesh the enmity, that is, the law of commandments contained in ordinances, so as to create in Himself one new man from the two, thus making peace, (Ephesians 2:14-15)

Lemuel's life was a picture of what Paul taught. He loved everyone in his church. The color of their skin didn't matter to him.

FAITHFUL TO THE END

Lemuel pastored in Vermont for thirty years. Then, from 1822 to 1833, he pastored in New York.

By this time, he was getting old. He thought more about heaven each day. Like the Apostle Paul, Lemuel wanted to "depart and be with Christ." He was ready to die.

In March 1833, Lemuel became sick. The illness grew worse over the next few months. He spent his time in prayer. He also read the Bible and thought about it a lot. He frequently spoke with friends and family. By July, it appeared that Lemuel was on the brink of eternity. He accepted this as God's will.

In his last days, Lemuel spoke to his children. "I am in God's hands. I trust His will. Remember Your Creator! Do not let the world distract you from eternity!"

Home of Lemuel Haynes

Before Lemuel died, he wrote a message for his tombstone. It says this:

> Here lies a poor sinner who deserved hell. He went into eternity trusting in Jesus Christ for salvation. He died believing in what he preached. He invites his children, and all who read this, to trust in Jesus Christ.

15

ASAHEL NETTLETON: PREACHING CHRIST TO AMERICA

On a beautiful fall evening, Asahel Nettleton watched the crowd dance. The year was 1800. Asahel lived in the state of Connecticut. Tonight the people of the town of Killingworth had gathered to celebrate. This was a night of feasting and dancing. The people held this feast every year. For many in town, it was their favorite time of year.

Asahel went to the dance that night. He hoped he would enjoy himself. But he found it hard to join in the fun. His mind was full of sad things. He kept thinking about death and God's judgment. What would happen when he died? He had sinned so many times in his life. How could he die with so many sins? What would happen to him?

Asahel left the dance and went home. His mind was still filled with burdens and doubts. The doubts he had that night did not end.

For the next few months, he kept thinking about sin and death. He thought about God's judgment and what would happen in eternity. He knew he was sinful. He said to himself, "Perhaps if I read my Bible more and do good things, I will feel better."

That is what Asahel did. He worked hard to be better. He hoped this would help. But it didn't. It only left him with more doubts. He wondered, "Is God real? Is the Bible really God's Word?"

Acting good didn't make Asahel feel better. Even though he went to church and read the Bible, this didn't take care of his sin problem. He needed a Savior. He needed someone to rescue him from his sins.

The Bible teaches that we can't be saved by our good works. We cannot pay for our own sins. The debt is too large. We can't pay for our sins by more good works. We all need a Savior who will take our sins away. We need a Savior who will obey God's law perfectly.

Asahel Nettleton (1783 - 1844)

That is what Jesus did. Through His death on the cross, He forgives us of all our sins when we believe. Through His perfect life, we receive His righteousness when we believe.

Have you ever obeyed God without sinning at all? No! If you try to obey Him for even one day, you will realize that you can't perfectly obey God's law.

For as by one man's disobedience many were made sinners, so also by one Man's obedience [Jesus' obedience] many will be made righteous. (Romans 5:19)

Thanks be to God! The Lord Jesus Christ is a perfect Savior!

ASAHEL BELIEVES IN JESUS

. . . if you confess with your mouth the Lord Jesus and believe in your heart that God has raised Him from the dead, you will be saved. (Romans 10:9)

After months of wrestling in his mind and heart, Asahel believed. The Holy Spirit of God opened his heart. He received the good news about Jesus. Filled with joy, he said this about his conversion:

Now God was lovely to me. My Savior Jesus was very precious. God's way of saving was something I did not like before. But now I delighted in the truth of God's Word. I now loved God's people. It was a joy to go to church. I found it delightful to read God's Word and pray.

Asahel was a new creation in Christ. He became a different kind of young man. New desires sprang up in his soul. He loved the things of God. He hated sin.

One of his new desires was to tell others about God. He wanted to reach the lost. He cared more about this than getting rich. He wrote, "I would rather see one soul saved than be the richest man in the world!" Asahel thought about going overseas. He could serve God in a faraway place. But he needed

Congregational church in Killingworth, Connecticut

to study first. He decided he would go to college and be trained.

But the Lord stopped Asahel's plans for a while. In 1802, a deadly plague swept through Killingworth. Asahel's father Samuel died. His younger brother David also died. Because Asahel was the oldest son, he had to provide for the family. He worked hard in the fields. All day long, he took care of the farm. At night, he studied. He still hoped he could bring the gospel to far-off lands one day.

After three years of hard work, Nettleton saved enough money to go to Yale College. He began his college studies in 1805. Not every student at Yale loved the Lord. Some cared more about becoming smart and rich than about God. But the Lord gave Asahel some Christian friends. He also talked with the other students and prayed for them. He tried to tell them about the Lord.

After four years, Asahel finished college. He started preaching God's Word in 1811. He still wanted to go overseas. But the Lord never let him do this. The Lord instead planned for him to preach God's Word in America.

ASAHEL PREACHES

"Is not My word like a fire?" says the Lord,
"And like a hammer that breaks the rock in pieces?" (Jeremiah 23:29)

Asahel preached God's Word in many churches in New England. He was an itinerant evangelist. God blessed him with the gift of preaching. He preached the Word in a way that honored God. He was serious about the Bible. He knew he was telling people eternal truth. God's Word had to be handled with great care. Asahel did not preach man's words. He didn't say things to make people like him. Instead, he worked hard to preach the truth. He wanted to preach God's Word faithfully.

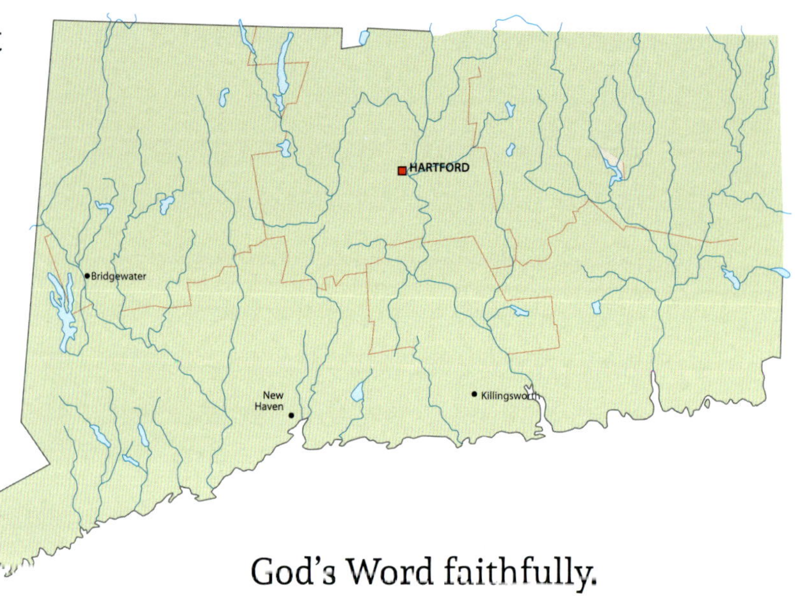

Itinerant Evangelist

A preacher who travels and preaches in many different places.

Asahel told men and women the truth about God and about themselves. He taught that sin was a great evil. But he also preached Jesus as the Lamb of

Illustration of Asahel Nettleton

God who takes away the sins of the world. He warned sinners about the dangers of hell. But he also told them the good news. He comforted them with the promise of God's mercy in Christ.

Asahel preached often. He also visited people in their homes. He held prayer meetings. The Lord added to the church through his work.

One year, in 1816, Asahel visited the town of Bridgewater. This town is in Connecticut. At a school building, a large crowd came to hear him preach. A man named "Mr. C" lived in Bridgewater. He did not believe in God. He was an atheist. The last thing Mr. C wanted to hear was God's Word preached! But Mr. C was curious that night. He thought Asahel must be a strange person. Perhaps it would be fun to watch him preach.

Atheist

A person who says that there is no god. The Bible says that atheists are fools (Psalm 14:1).

Mr. C took a stroll and arrived at the school building. Hundreds crowded in to hear Asahel. Mr. C did not enter the building. He stood at the door and listened.

Asahel boldly proclaimed the gospel. He warned his hearers about their sin. He called to the audience, "Repent, and believe the gospel! Believe in the Lord Jesus, and you will be saved!"

At first Mr. C did not like the message. But as he heard the sermon, his heart softened. The Holy Spirit opened Mr. C's eyes. By the end of the message, he repented. He cried out, "Save me, Lord, for I am a sinful man!" Mr. C wept in front of everyone. The Lord saved him.

This is an example of the Holy Spirit's power. The Holy Spirit can wake up dead sinners. He can give them spiritual life. Asahel knew that it was God who saves. Asahel did not have any power to save people. He said, "God is the only One who can save. If a sinner gets saved, it only happens by God's sovereign power."

ASAHEL GETS SICK

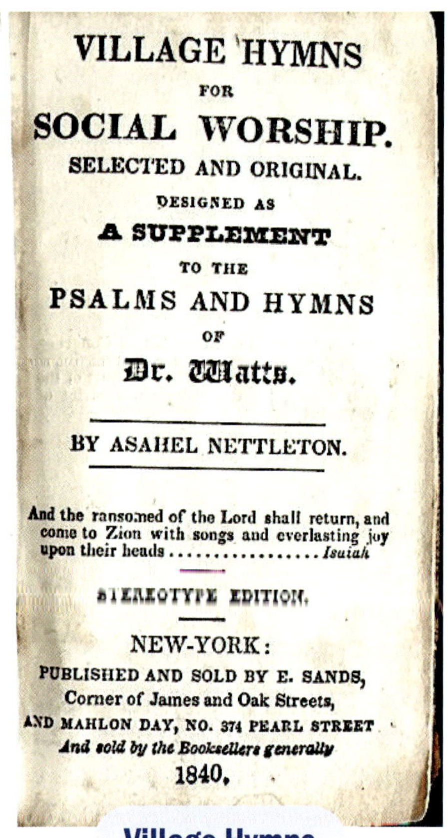
VILLAGE HYMNS
FOR
SOCIAL WORSHIP.
SELECTED AND ORIGINAL.
DESIGNED AS
A SUPPLEMENT
TO THE
PSALMS AND HYMNS
OF
Dr. Watts.

BY ASAHEL NETTLETON.

And the ransomed of the Lord shall return, and come to Zion with songs and everlasting joy upon their heads .... *Isaiah*

STEREOTYPE EDITION.

NEW-YORK:
PUBLISHED AND SOLD BY E. SANDS,
Corner of James and Oak Streets,
AND MAHLON DAY, NO. 374 PEARL STREET
And sold by the Booksellers generally
1840.

Village Hymns

The LORD will strengthen him on his bed of illness;
You will sustain him on his sickbed. (Psalm 41:3)

By 1822, thousands had been saved by hearing Asahel preach. He preached thousands of times throughout America.

In October 1822, the Lord sent Asahel a difficult trial. He became sick with typhus. Typhus is a very deadly disease. Asahel almost died.

But after a few months, Asahel began to get better. Still, his health was weak for the next two years. He could not preach very often. But he did not waste his time. He said, "I will serve the Lord even here in bed!"

Asahel spent two years creating a new hymnbook. He believed the American church needed a new hymnal. He collected new and old songs for the book. He even wrote some of the music for the songs. In 1824, he published his new hymnbook. It was called Village Hymns. Even though he was sick, Asahel didn't waste time. His hymnbook was a blessing to many Christians.

ASAHEL KEEPS ON PREACHING

Soon, Asahel's health was much better. He began traveling to preach more. He preached throughout America. He also defended the church from false teaching. At this time, many of the churches were not faithful to the Bible. Asahel helped people understand what the Bible said. He showed them that some preachers were teaching false things.

God used Asahel to reach many people with the message of salvation. Thousands were saved. Perhaps as many as 30,000 came to faith through his preaching. Of course, Asahel did not save these people. It is God who saves. But the Lord does use servants like Asahel to bring the message to lost people. God was glorified by this. The Lord brought in a great harvest of souls.

Elizabeth Park, Hartford, Connecticut

Hartford, Connecticut

In 1833, Asahel decided to start a school. In Hartford, he started a college for training young men. There, he taught many young men about the ministry. He discipled many young men. All the students loved him.

After about ten years, Asahel's time to go be with the Lord drew near. In 1844, he became sick. In May of that year, his friends gathered at his bedside. Asahel said, "I am not afraid to die, my friends. I have peace with God through my Lord Jesus Christ."

On May 16, Asahel spoke his last words. To his friends he said, "It is sweet to trust in the Lord." He then went to be with the Lord. Asahel gave his entire life for the cause of Jesus. He was faithful to the end.

Thanks be to God for faithful servants like Asahel Nettleton! May we, like him, be used for God's glory.

Rio Grande River

MELINDA RANKIN: TWENTY YEARS IN MEXICO

16

"You are worthy to take the scroll,
And to open its seals;
For You were slain,
And have redeemed us to God by Your blood
Out of every tribe and tongue and people and nation." (Revelation 5:9)

The mighty Rio Grande River divides Mexico from the United States. There are many towns sitting on this river border. One of them is Brownsville, Texas. The Rio Grande passes right through the city. If you visit Brownsville, you will be within sight of the border. From this city, you can cross the border into Mexico.

Many things have happened in Brownsville. This city has been the site of many battles. History books often tell about the battles that took place there. But Christians should remember something else about this town. From here, the Bible crossed the border into Mexico. God raised up a woman of great courage to do this. Her name was Melinda Rankin.

For twenty years, Melinda served the people of Mexico. She was a woman. She wasn't a strong person. She was weak in the world's eyes. But God uses weak people to do mighty thing. Melinda wrote, "God can work His own purposes with weak instruments." This is exactly what He did. God did great things in Mexico through people like Melinda.

FROM NEW ENGLAND TO MEXICO

All the ends of the world
Shall remember and turn to the LORD,
And all the families of the nations
Shall worship before You. (Psalm 22:27)

Melinda Rankin was born in New Hampshire. This is a long way from Mexico. Why did she leave her home? What made her decide to give her life to Mexico?

God put this desire in her heart. When Melinda was a little girl, God saved her. The Holy Spirit gave her new life. She trusted in Christ from a young age. From that point on, she wanted to teach others about Christ. God gave her a gift. She was good at teaching. In 1840, she became a teacher. She helped to teach young girls. She worked at a school in Kentucky. She also taught in Mississippi.

In 1846, a war started between Mexico and the United States. It was called the Mexican-American War. In 1848, the war ended. After the war was over, soldiers returned to their homes. Melinda didn't know much about the people in Mexico. But she learned about them from the soldiers who came home after the war. Most Americans didn't like the Mexican people. After all, they had been at war for two years! The war was over. But in many ways, Mexico was still an enemy.

Melinda's heart ached for the Mexican people. She knew they needed the Bible. They had never read God's Word. But who would take on this task? Who would take the Bible to them? Melinda wrote, "I learned that Mexico was a country right on our border. The light of the Bible had never come there. A pure Christian faith was missing from that land."

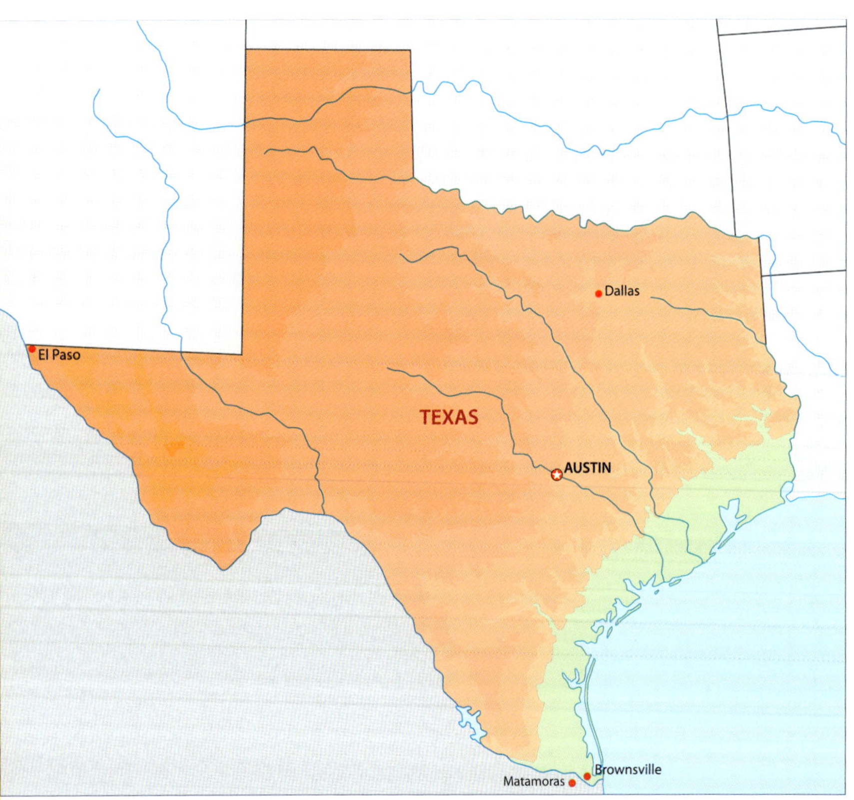

Most people in Mexico belonged to the Roman Catholic Church. They went to church, but the priests of the church didn't allow them to read the Bible. Mexicans could not learn the true gospel. The Roman church

Battle during the Mexican-American War

wasn't teaching the people about God. They were leading the people astray.

"These people need the Bible," Melinda said to herself. But she seemed to be the only one who wanted to go. No one else wanted to journey to Mexico. Even if no one else would go, Melinda decided that she would go. She would take the Bible to Mexico.

But this was not an easy thing to do. Most of the people in the United States didn't like the idea. Mexico was an enemy land. It would be dangerous to go there. Why would anyone risk their life for Mexicans?

Melinda was a student of the Bible. In the Bible, she read that Jesus died for every tribe, tongue, and nation. That meant that Mexico should also be won for Jesus. She began her journey to Texas. Her goal was to get into Mexico. She did not know how she would get there. By faith, she began her journey.

TEACHING AND GIVING AWAY BIBLES

The word of God is living and active. It is sharper than any sword that has two edges. It cuts deep enough to separate soul from spirit. It can separate joints from bones. It judges the thoughts and purposes of the heart. (Hebrews 4:12 NIRV)

In 1852, Melinda moved to Brownsville. She could see Mexico across the river. On the other side of the river was the town of Matamoras, Mexico.

Living alone as a woman in Brownsville was dangerous. This town was part of the wild west. Melinda might have been robbed or attacked. But she wasn't afraid. Christ's servants are never alone. Melinda knew that "the name of the Lord is a strong tower" (Proverbs 18:10). She knew that God was watching over her. She could trust Him to take care of her.

Melinda did not go to Mexico yet. She started a school for Mexican girls in Texas. When the school started, it only had five girls. But it grew quickly. Many of these girls were orphans. Melinda was like a mother to them. She taught them how to read and write. More importantly, she taught them the Bible.

At this time, it was against the law to teach the Bible in Mexico. But Melinda's school was in Texas. It was safe to teach the Bible there. That is why Melinda started in Texas. But she did not want to stop at the border. Mexico itself was on her heart.

Melinda wrote, "I taught the girls that the Bible was God's book. What God taught in the Bible we must obey. Soon, the children taught this to their parents. Then the parents wanted to learn more about the Bible."

It was illegal to send Bibles into Mexico. This did not stop Melinda. She started sending Bibles across the border. God's Word is like a hammer that breaks through rock (Jeremiah 23:29). Melinda knew that God's Word could soften hard hearts. She wrote, "People carried dozens of Bibles over the river. They gave them out to the people. The people gladly received them. I become convinced that good would be done. It seemed like a small attack upon the enemy's camp. But the missiles we sent are powerful. I knew that damage would be done to the kingdom of darkness."

Melinda Rankin teaching schoolgirls

Satan's kingdom was under attack. But when the evil one is attacked, he fights back. The evil one wants to stop God's Word. Bibles were brought over the border. Mexicans were reading God's Word for the first time. Roman Catholic priests got upset. They didn't want the people to read the Bible. They tried to stop this. Whenever they could, they took the Bibles and burned them.

Melinda's school in Brownsville grew and grew. She taught hundreds of girls. She kept sending Bibles into Mexico. She also sent **tracts**. A tract is a small booklet that talks about God or the Bible. Melinda needed help to pay for these things. She traveled around the United States. She told people about her work and raised money for it. It was not easy to find people who wanted to help. Many Americans did not want to support her. Some people didn't care about the lost souls in Mexico. When Melinda asked one pastor for support, he shook his head. He told her: "It would be better for us to send bullets and gunpowder to Mexico rather than Bibles." This was not a godly response. But not everyone thought this way. God sent generous helpers for Melinda. He provided the money she needed.

God sent all the money that the school needed. Melinda was able to make the school even bigger. Soon she could build a new building in the city. It was a three-story school building. There Melinda and other teachers taught the Bible faithfully. Melinda, with the help of others, went door to door to all the homes in Brownsville. They offered a Spanish Bible to every family. Almost every family gladly took the Bibles. But the Mexican families had to keep the Bibles hidden. Otherwise, the priests would come and burn them. For this reason, many families would only read their Bibles at night.

More trouble came to the mission work in 1860. A civil war started in the United States. The southern and northern states started fighting each other. This made things very hard for the school. Texas was a southern state. But Melinda often traveled to northern states to tell people about her school. Many people in New York gave money for her work. But New York was a northern state. How could she reach them now that the war was going on? Would they still be able to send her money to help with the school?

Melinda didn't know the answers to these questions. But she trusted God. She knew God could provide for the school. He could send money to pay for the Bibles that she was giving away. The Lord opened doors for Melinda. She began to raise money in the southern states. She also found a way to get to New York.

Monterrey, Mexico

For a time, she left Brownsville. She went across the border to Mexico. Then she opened a school in Matamoras. Now she could begin to serve in Mexico.

Two battles were fought in Brownsville during the war. The school building was damaged in one of them. But after the war ended, people rebuilt the school. This was a hard time for the city. But Melinda kept working.

Meanwhile, things were changing in Mexico. A violent revolution was going on. The people in charge of the country were thrown out. Then new people started to rule. The Lord used this change to open the way for more Bibles to come into the land. Soon, more missionaries arrived. They took the Bible to the people of Mexico. Melinda helped them.

Preachers of the Word came from the United States. Melinda records, “They went from house to house. They went from ranch to ranch. Many souls were brought into the light of the gospel.”

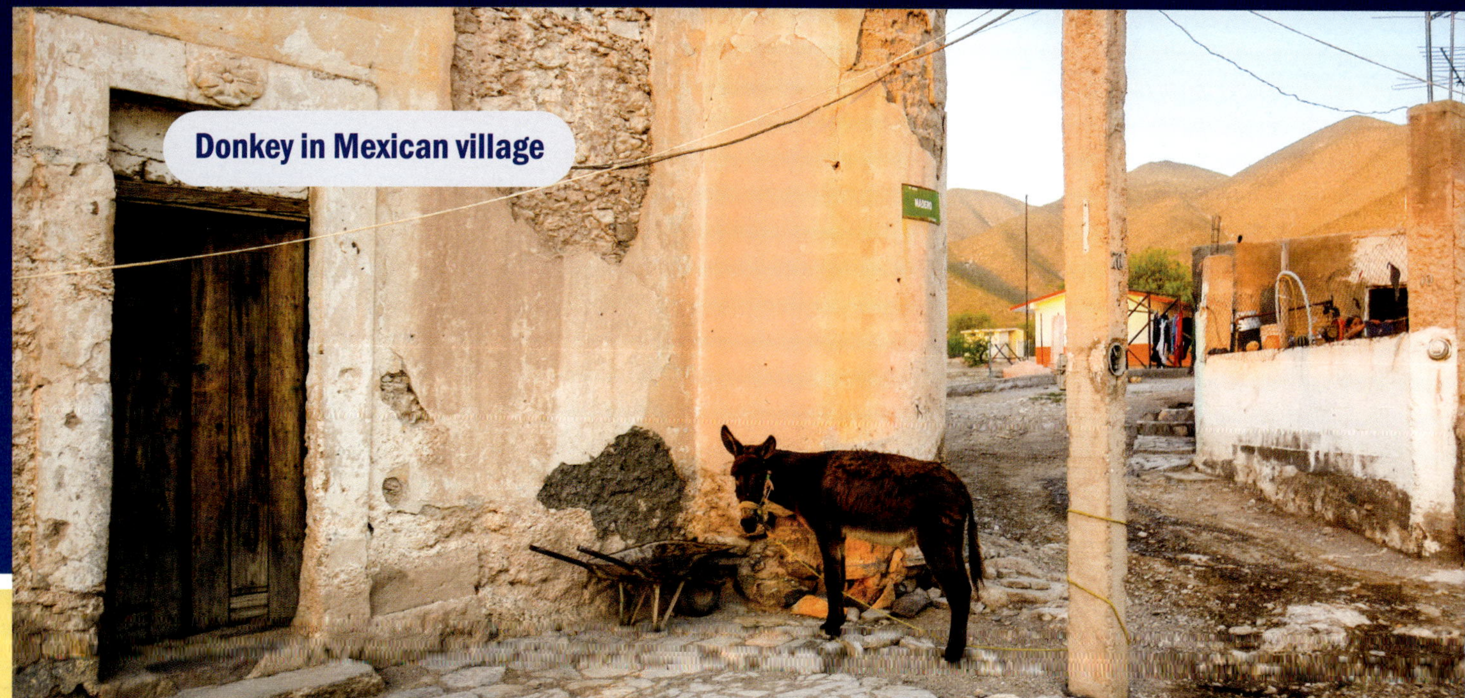
Donkey in Mexican village

More and more Mexicans learned about Christ. God saved them. Soon, they began to start churches. Mexican pastors began sharing the gospel. The Word was going forth. No human power could stop it.

Melinda stayed busy with her work. She taught children. She prayed. She raised support. She gave away Bibles. Then, in 1872, she retired from her labors. She returned home to the United States. But her work was not over. She traveled across the states. She wanted to tell people about the work in Mexico. She wanted people to help with the work. Her love for Mexico was obvious. She gave her life to reach Mexico for Christ.

BASIC FACTS ABOUT MEXICO	
Total population:	131 million
Total area:	761,000 square miles
Capital:	Mexico City
Official language:	Spanish
Primary religion:	Roman Catholic

PRAYER POINTS: MEXICO

Now, take some time to pray for the people of Mexico.

- **Pray for an End to Crime**
  Mexico has a large drug trade. Because of this, there is a lot of stealing, kidnapping, and murder. Government and police try to stop this. But they can't stop it all. The people of Mexico need new hearts. They need Christ. Pray that God would transform this country. Pray that crime would come to an end.

- **Pray for Bible Translation Work**
  Spanish is the main language of Mexico. But there are about sixty-eight other languages. These languages are spoken by tribal groups. Not all of them have a Bible in their own language. Ask God to send His Word to these people. Pray for someone to translate the Bible for these tribes.

- **Pray for Living Faith**
  Most Mexicans know something about Christ. But many have not been taught God's Word. They do not have true faith in Jesus Christ. Pray that Mexicans would know the true Christ and the true gospel.
  friend you know. Ask God to change their hearts.

Agave Field in Mexico

Cape Horn, South America

CAPTAIN ALLEN GARDINER: TIERRA DEL FUEGO

17

But you shall receive power when the Holy Spirit has come upon you; and you shall be witnesses to Me in Jerusalem, and in all Judea and Samaria, and to the end of the earth." (Acts 1:8)

Antarctica is the continent at the bottom of the world. It is a giant landmass covered in ice. Not many people live there. It is far too cold and icy. Just eighty miles north of Antarctica is the tip of South America. This tip is called Cape Horn. Because it is so far south, it is cold too. This part of South America is called Tierra del Fuego.

In Spanish, "Tierra del Fuego" means "Land of Fire." A Spanish explorer gave this land its name. His name was Ferdinand Magellan. In 1520, he explored this region. He noticed many fires on the coastline. The natives used these fires to stay warm. This is why he called this land "Land of Fire."

For sailors, Tierra del Fuego was a hard place to explore. Here, the ocean was swept with strong winds. Icebergs brought many dangers. But this did not stop men from sailing these seas.

They needed to get from the Atlantic to the Pacific Ocean. For hundreds of years, ships passed through the region. It was the only way to get from one ocean to the other.

Other dangers met passing ships. The native peoples of these islands were violent. Ships that passed by these shores tried to avoid the natives living there. Many people thought these natives were too savage to ever change. "They are so ugly!" men would exclaim. These natives were called Fuegians. Most of them did not wear clothes. Other people found this shocking. Tierra del Fuego is a cold place. But the Fuegians walked around with no clothing. Many of them slept in the open air. They made their beds right on the ground.

Fuegian

A word used to describe the people groups living in Tierra del Fuego. Many tribes lived in this area and were called by the same name.

The Fuegians did not seem to be very smart. But Europeans were most shocked by how these people acted. The natives stole and killed. They did very wicked things. They often left their own children and did not care for them.

HMS *Beagle* in the Strait of Magellan

Once a famous man came to Tierra del Fuego. His name was Charles Darwin. He traveled the seas on a ship called the HMS *Beagle*. On these journeys, Darwin saw many animals. He studied them and wrote down many things about them.

When Darwin visited Tierra del Fuego, he saw the natives there. He was impressed by them. They were skillful in hunting. They could live in cold weather. But Darwin thought these people were not the same as he was. He believed they were not as human as he was. He called them "among the lowest" forms of human. He said they were close to the monkeys in the jungle. Many other people felt the same way about the Fuegians.

Darwin believed in **evolution**. This is a belief that says all human beings came from apes. This is a lie. The Bible teaches us the truth about human beings. It tells us that God made man different than the animals. God made mankind in His own image. We aren't like monkeys or any other animal. All humans are made in the image of God.

Charles Darwin (1809-1882)

But some people didn't believe this. They looked at the Fuegians and said, "They are not human in the same way that we are." Even the language that these natives spoke sounded very strange to the rest of the world. Their words sounded like grunting instead of speech. It didn't sound like a real human language at all.

For all these reasons, people looked down on the Fuegians. They didn't show love to these natives. For centuries, people tried to stay away from them. Meanwhile, the Fuegians lived and died without knowing about Jesus Christ. No one had ever told them about Him. It would take true faith and love to reach them.

No one loved these natives. But the Lord was merciful to them. He sent a man named Allen Gardiner. Allen would bring the gospel to the Fuegians.

CAPTAIN GARDINER'S COURAGE

Allen Francis Gardiner was an officer in the British Royal Navy. He spent over twenty years at sea. By the time he was forty years old, he held the rank of captain. He was a gifted naval officer. He had a good future to look forward to in the navy. But he decided to leave his career. Instead of serving in the navy, he would give his life to mission work.

Captain Allen Gardiner (1794-1851)

On his voyages around the world, Captain Gardiner learned many things. He learned much about native tribes. He saw their need for Jesus. He longed to take the gospel to those who had never heard of Christ. He spent a few years in South Africa and then in South America. Then he set his sights on Tierra del Fuego. It was a lonely and dangerous place to go. No one had ever dared to live among the Fuegians. Allen Gardiner would be the first.

Schooner (pronounced "skoo-ner")
A small sailing vessel.

Gardiner piloted a schooner to Tierra del Fuego in 1842. But he did not stay long on the islands. The natives were unfriendly. Quickly Gardiner realized that his life was in danger. He knew he would need help if he wanted to reach these people. He couldn't do this dangerous work alone. He returned to England to raise support and find helpers.

In 1844, Gardiner formed a group to help bring the gospel to the natives. He named it the South American Missionary Society. It started out very small. Not many people came to help. But that did not matter. The Lord can do great things with a little.

Captain Gardiner went to Tierra del Fuego many times. He longed to see the Fuegians saved from their sins. He knew that only the blood of Christ could save them.

For many years, Gardiner worked. But little progress was made. The weather was cold. The natives were fierce. They did not want to hear the good news. Gardiner and those with him were discouraged. But they didn't give up. They knew they had to persevere.

In 1850, Captain Gardiner made a final voyage to Tierra del Fuego. He and the people with him landed on Picton Island. They brought two small boats. The boats held enough food for six months. Tragically, they did not take enough gunpowder to hunt. Food quickly ran out. A ship with new supplies was on its way, but it didn't arrive in time.

After the food ran out, Captain Gardiner knew he and his men would die. But he wasn't afraid. Taking out his Bible, he wrote a note for the people on the supply ship. He wanted them to know what had happened. He wrote:

Yet a little while. Then I will go to the Almighty. I will sing His praises. I am not hungry or thirsty, even though I have not had food for five days. Allen Gardiner. September 6, 1851.

When he finished his note, Captain Gardiner picked up his Bible. He knew he would die soon. But first, he would read from God's Word. His hope was in Christ. He trusted in God. Even though he was dying, he knew that God would send others to bring the gospel to the Fuegians.

When the supply ship arrived, Captain Gardiner and his men were dead. But God was not finished. He would still bring His light to Tierra del Fuego.

MISSIONARY WORK CONTINUES

And let us not grow weary while doing good, for in due season we shall reap if we do not lose heart. (Galatians 6:9)

Captain Gardiner spent many years in Tierra del Fuego. The natives

The *Allen Gardiner* navigating through Tierra del Fuego

treated him badly. They threatened to kill him. His life was hard. But he endured all this with joy. He stayed here because of his love for the Fuegians. He wanted to bring them to Jesus. But not a single native changed during this time. Not a single one repented. None of them trusted in Christ.

Did Captain Gardiner waste his life? Some people thought he did. But others knew the truth. They knew that he had given his life for the cause of Christ. They were filled with sadness when they heard about his death. What would happen to the mission now?

This was a sad time, but it was part of God's plan. God had a purpose in what happened. The captain's death inspired others to follow him. Christians in England would not allow his life and death to be wasted. A pastor named George Despard helped the mission go on. He said, "With God's help, the mission will continue."

In 1855, a new ship left England. It was bound for South America. This new ship would help the mission. It was called the Allen Gardiner. On board was Captain Gardiner's son. His name was also Allen Gardiner.

The missionaries built a home base on a nearby island. It was called Keppel Island. This is only about 400 miles from Tierra del Fuego. From this island, they could make shorter journeys to meet with the natives.

Keppel Island is part of the Falkland Islands. These islands lie off the coast of Argentina.

Then they tried a new strategy. First, they worked to learn the language. They visited Tierra del Fuego. Some of the Fuegians were curious about these strange new people. They decided to go with them to Keppel Island. This helped the mission in two ways. First, the missionaries learned the language from their new friends. Second, they were able to teach the Bible to these curious natives. Fuegians on Keppel Island

King penguin and penguin chicks on the Falkland Islands

Lighthouse in Ushuaia

attended worship each Sunday. They also learned how to read and write. Slowly, God's Spirit began to work in their hearts.

The next step was to take the Fuegians back to their homes. When these natives went home, they shared the good news of Jesus. Soon, the gospel took root.

In 1869, a mission station was built in Tierra del Fuego. Three years later, thirty-six native believers were baptized. Soon, others were turning to Christ. The peoples of the islands began to change. The mission station became a beacon of hope. In fact, sailors passing through the area began to stop there. They knew they would be safe near the mission station.

Later, Charles Darwin heard the news. He heard what had happened to the natives. In shock, he wrote, "I did not believe that all the missionaries in the world could have made these people honest." Even Charles Darwin was amazed! This is a picture of the power of Christ's gospel.

Today, Tierra del Fuego is part of two countries. Part of it is in Chile, and part of it is in Argentina. Much has changed since the 1800s. The mission station is now the city of Ushuaia. It is one of the largest cities in the region.

BASIC FACTS ABOUT ARGENTINA

ARGENTINE REPUBLIC	
Total population:	45 million
Total area:	1,073,000 square miles
Capital:	Buenos Aires
Official language:	Spanish
Primary religion:	Roman Catholic

PRAYER POINTS: ARGENTINA

Now, take some time to pray for the people of Argentina.

- **Praise God for the Growth of the Church**
  God's church is growing. In 1980, there were around one million evangelical Christians in Argentina. By 2010, the number was closer to 3.7 million. Let us praise God for building Christ's church.
- **Thank God for Prison Ministries**
  Many prisoners in Argentina have become Christians while in prison. About twenty-five percent are now Christians. The Lord has used prisons to humble some people. One prison is run by Christians. It has about 250 pastors who minister to the inmates.
- **Pray for More Godly Pastors**
  The churches of Argentina need more leaders. The fields are ready for harvest. But more laborers are needed. Pray that God would raise up faithful shepherds to lead and teach His people.

Sunrise over Hudson Bay

18 JOHN HORDEN: TAKING THE GOSPEL TO HUDSON BAY

Praise the LORD from the earth,
You great sea creatures and all the depths;
Fire and hail, snow and clouds;
Stormy wind, fulfilling His word. (Psalm 148:7-8)

Ice could be seen in every direction. Loud cracks were heard as ice buckled and broke beneath the ship's hull. Slowly, the ship sailed south. It was August 1851. Summer had come, but Hudson Bay was still full of ice. In the distance, a beluga whale surfaced for air. A moment later, the whale slipped back into the frigid waters.

A journey through Hudson Bay was a treacherous trip. Ships could easily be wrecked by the ice. They could also become trapped, with no hope of sailing free.

Aboard the ship were John and Elizabeth Horden. This British couple had sailed all the way from England. They were headed to Moose Fort. Moose Fort sat on a small island in the southern part of Hudson Bay. There the Cree Indians lived. And there John and Elizabeth would live for over forty years. This would be their home from 1851 until 1893.

John recorded what the journey was like in his journals. He wrote, "We made slow progress with all the ice. On August 12, we sailed six miles in five hours. But then the ship came to a halt. We were stuck fast in the ice."

For a week, the ship was locked in ice. "We played ball on the ice while we waited to break through," John wrote.

Finally, on August 26, John and Elizabeth safely arrived at Moose Fort. The long voyage had lasted more than two months. Now they had reached their new home.

A ship stuck in the ice of Hudson Bay, 1837

EARLY LABORS

John and Elizabeth settled into their little cabin at Moose Fort. Before long, their ship left again for England.

Once a year, the settlers at Moose Fort eagerly awaited the next ship. Usually, around August or September, supplies arrived.

It was difficult to travel around Moose Fort. There were no roads here. If you wanted to go somewhere, you needed a canoe, snowshoes, or sled dogs!

Moose Fort was home to Cree Indians and many English settlers. John had come to be their new pastor. But he had a problem. He didn't know the Cree language. So, each day, he diligently talked with the natives. Slowly he began to learn their strange words.

John was a hard worker. The Cree were impressed by his progress. After a few months, he preached a sermon in Cree. After only eight months, John was able to speak the language clearly.

The next step was to translate the Bible for the Cree. John began to work right away. But this was not an easy task. He would work on this project for the rest of his life.

John translated the Gospels first. Then he translated a book of prayers and a songbook. But he had no way to print the books! There was no printing press in Moose Fort.

John sent copies of his books on a ship going back to England. In his letter, he asked for one thousand copies to be printed. But instead of sending copies, men from England sent John a printing press of his own. This was a valuable tool. Yet John still had a problem. He didn't know how to use the press.

The printing press did not come with an instruction manual. But John was resourceful. He studied the mechanism for days. One day, settlers in Moose Fort heard him running through the camp. "Come see how this works!" he exclaimed.

John was waving papers above his head. He had figured out how to work the printing press. John and his friends at Moose Fort began printing thousands of books. God used these translations to spread the faith.

Location of Moose Factory and Churchill

WILDERNESS JOURNEYS

But in all things we commend ourselves as ministers of God: in much patience, in tribulations, in needs, in distresses, in stripes, in imprisonments, in tumults, in labors, in sleeplessness, in fastings. (2 Corinthians 6:4-5)

The Church of England sent John to Hudson Bay. They wanted him to preach to the people at Moose Fort. But they didn't want him to only work in Moose Fort. They asked him to work with people all over Moosonee. This was a massive region. Some of John's journeys took him over 500 miles away from his home.

In the winter, John traveled with sled dogs. Or he would snowshoe. In the summer, he would travel across the bay by canoe. Hudson Bay contained many outposts. John visited each of them.

John's wilderness journeys were difficult and dangerous. In his journal he records these trips. One of these trips led him to Fort Churchill. Churchill is on the western side of Hudson Bay. It is called the polar bear capital of the world. Few places are as cold as Churchill.

John's journey was long, difficult, and very cold. Here are some entries from his journal.

February 2, 1880. Set out after breakfast for Churchill. Cold is severe. Wind is high. We are constantly stopped by thick ice.

February 6, 1880. The weather has not gotten better. But we must proceed.

Illustration of John Horden traveling by sled dog

Food for men and dogs is limited. We must go on. Temperature today was 38° below zero.

February 8, 1880. At 11AM, we could go no further. It was too cold. Temperature reached 46° below zero.

Polar bears on Hudson Bay

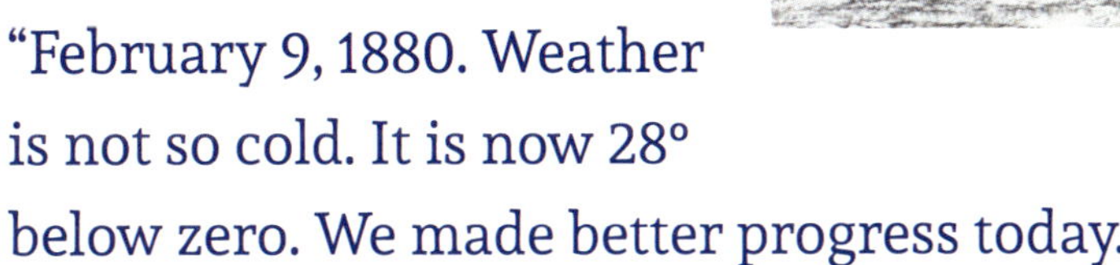

"February 9, 1880. Weather is not so cold. It is now 28° below zero. We made better progress today.

At last, John and his companions reached Churchill. There, John led the settlers in worship. He preached God's Word. But he couldn't stay long. Later on, he ordained a pastor to serve there. This man would serve the church in Churchill permanently.

CHALLENGES AND VICTORIES

In this you greatly rejoice, though now for a little while, if need be, you have been grieved by various trials, that the genuineness of your faith, being much more precious than gold that perishes, though it is tested by fire, may be found to praise, honor, and glory at the revelation of Jesus Christ. (1 Peter 1:6-7)

Life on Hudson Bay was not a life of comfort and ease. John and his wife faced many trials. Extremely cold weather was a part of daily life. Other troubles came as well.

John and the other settlers often ran low on food. Some winters, John and others at Moose Fort had to eat less. One year, the ship from England never

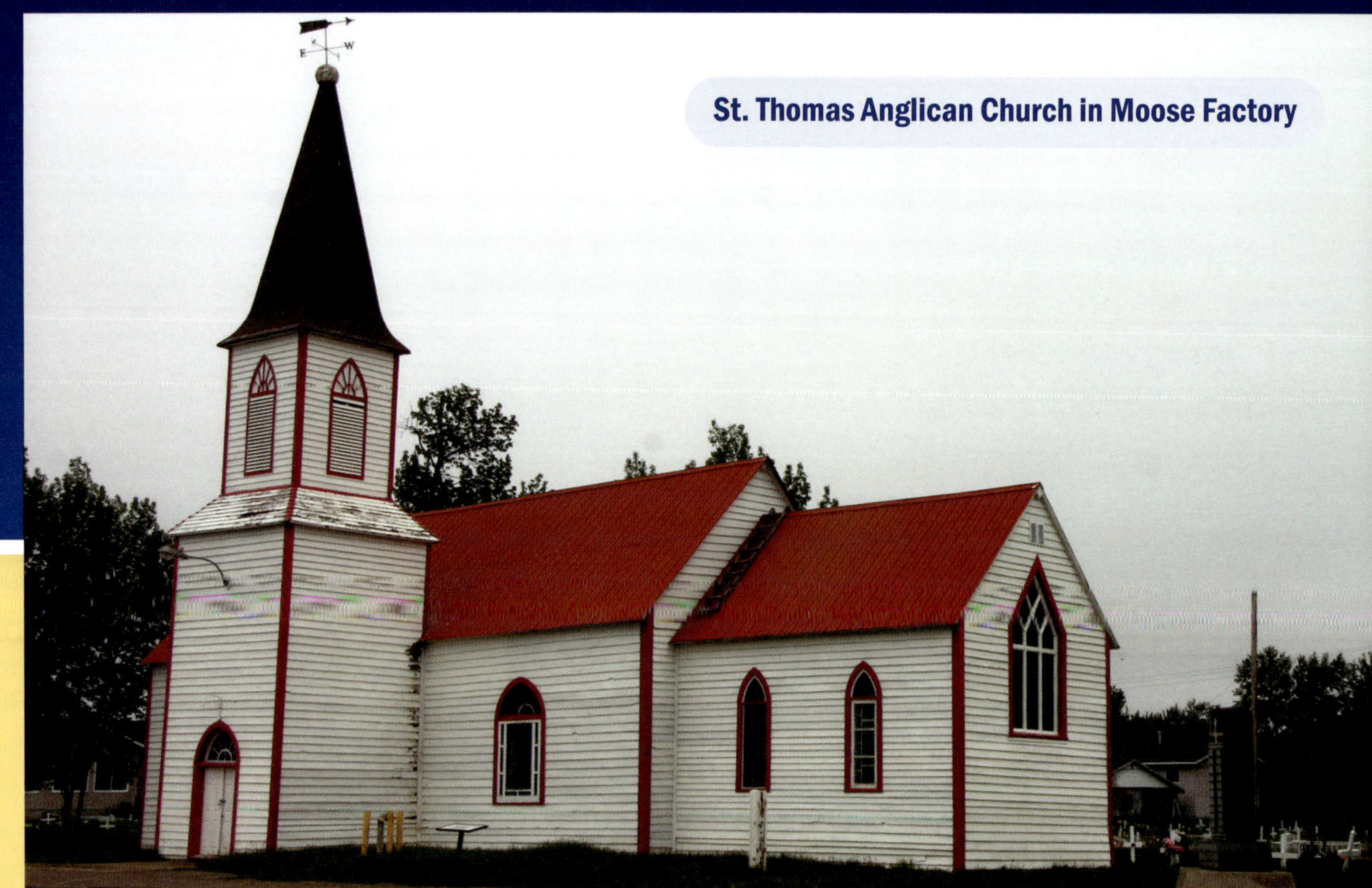
St. Thomas Anglican Church in Moose Factory

arrived. It had hit ice in the bay and sunk. The people of Moose Fort were grieved by this loss. Their yearly supply of food was gone. Many lives were lost as well.

The yearly ice melt in spring and summer could also be dangerous. One winter, snowstorms piled masses of snow on the island. When summer arrived the next year, Moose Fort was deluged with water. As the ice continued to melt, the rivers swelled.

John recorded what happened:

"On the night of May 21, we heard the noise of distant thunders. The river was swelling from melting ice. Soon, the alarm bell rang in Moose Fort. Danger was approaching. My house was exposed to the coming flood. The river rose twenty feet above its normal level. Soon, every house on the island was completely covered by water. After the flood ended, I found that my kitchen had been under five feet of water."

God was merciful. No one died in the flood. Everyone escaped the town before the waters consumed Moose Fort.

In 1860, another flood struck. The surging waters were strong. They lifted the church building from its foundation and carried it away. After the flood was over, the building was found a mile away from where it had been built.

As you can see, John lived in difficult conditions. But because he was serving Jesus, he was a joyful man. John once said, "The happiest man is the man who is diligent in serving his Master Jesus."

For over forty years, John happily served the Lord Jesus at Hudson Bay. He endured challenge after challenge. The Lord was very merciful to the Indians and Eskimos of Hudson Bay. Thousands came to saving faith in Jesus. In a barren, cold land, a spiritual harvest of souls took place during John Horden's ministry.

Arctic fox near Hudson Bay

Rio de Janeiro, Brazil

19 DR. ROBERT KALLEY: THE WOLF FROM SCOTLAND

He [Jesus] sent them to preach the kingdom of God and to heal the sick. (Luke 9:2)

A large crowd gathered in the town square. Above them, the city's cathedral towered silently. Violent and angry shouts filled the streets. At the center of the throng, the local Roman Catholic priest shouted above the noise of the crowd. "Long live the Holy Mother Church! Death to the Bible-readers! Death to Dr. Kalley, the wolf from Scotland!"

Ever since Dr. Kalley first arrived on Madeira, people tried to stop him. Persecution was constant. But in August 1846 at the cathedral, the people's anger boiled over. What had Dr. Kalley done? Why did the angry mob want to hurt him?

MISSION TO MADEIRA

The entrance of Your words gives light;
It gives understanding to the simple. (Psalm 119:130)

Dr. Robert Kalley was a doctor from Scotland. He traveled to the beautiful island of Madeira to care for his wife. She was often ill. The cold winters of Scotland were difficult for her. Dr. Kalley thought, "The warmer weather of

Madeira will be good for her."

Dr. Kalley and his wife Margaret planned to stay on the island for the winter. Then they would return to Scotland. But instead, they remained on Madeira. They lived there for eight years.

Dr. Kalley was a gifted doctor. He cared for many sick people. He also shared God's Word. He prayed with the sick. He read the Bible to them. He even wrote Bible verses on the medicine bottles he gave out. Dr. Kalley was not just a doctor. He was also an evangelist. "It is my duty to proclaim the truth. Madeira needs the gospel!" he wrote.

MADEIRA

This is what got him into trouble. Dr. Kalley taught the Bible. He taught the true gospel of Christ. But the people of Madeira were Roman Catholic. The church leaders there became angry at what Dr. Kalley taught. Many of the people began reading the Bible for themselves. Many of them stopped coming to the cathedral. They went to hear Dr. Kalley preach instead. This made the priests very upset.

Robert Reid Kalley (1809-1888)

The people of Madeira loved to read the Bible. Finally, they could read God's Word for themselves! Dr. Kalley wrote, "When I first came to Madeira, I met few who had ever seen a Bible. They did not even know there were four gospels. But they had gone to the Catholic church their whole life."

By 1842, thousands gathered to hear the Bible. They listened as Dr. Kalley preached

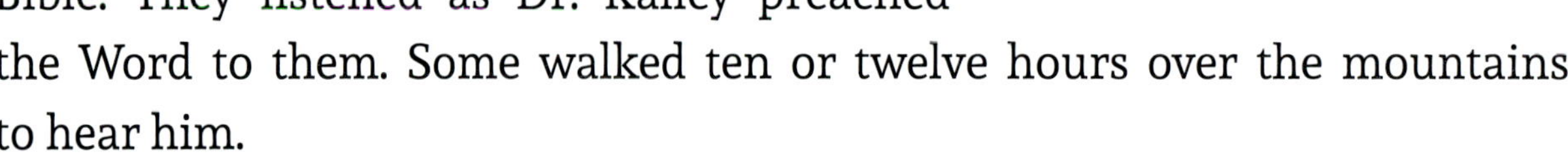
the Word to them. Some walked ten or twelve hours over the mountains to hear him.

Dr. Kalley also opened schools on Madeira. There, he and his wife Margaret taught reading and writing. Many people did not know how to read.

Roman Catholic Cathedral in Funchal, Madeira

Even many of the adults had never learned. It was a blessing to learn this skill. The main textbook of the school was the Bible. Dr. Kalley taught Bible stories in Portuguese. This is the language that was used on the island. He also translated Psalms and hymns into this language. The people of Madeira sang as they worked and traveled. On the streets of the cities, the Psalms of the Bible were heard. Dr. Kalley and his wife were making an impact.

In August 1843, Dr. Kalley was arrested. Guards led him to prison.

"What have I done wrong?" Dr. Kalley asked.

"You have broken the law," the guard explained. "On this island, we follow the Roman Catholic teaching. No one is allowed to teach any other religion here."

Dr. Kalley had taught the Bible. Because of this, he was imprisoned. He spent six months in prison. But the British government did all they could to help. After six months, they were able to set him free.

1845 is a special year for Madeira. In that year, the first Protestant church on the island began. As the church grew, suffering followed. The authorities tried to stop the church. They sent converts to prison. In October 1845, twenty-eight believers were put in prison. What was their crime? They were reading the Bible and praying together.

A year later, an angry mob gathered to attack the church. They ransacked the houses of church members. They stole animals and possessions. They burned down houses. But they weren't content with this. In August 1846, they searched the island for Dr. Kalley. "Long live the Roman Catholic Church! Death to the wolf! Death to Kalley!"

The mob searched for Dr. Kalley, but they couldn't find him. He was not at home. He was hidden in a nearby house. A ship was waiting for him at the port. But how would he get on board safely?

The Christians made a plan. They would disguise Dr. Kalley as a sick person. Quickly they placed him on a hammock. Then they covered him with a sheet. Quietly, four men carried him in the hammock. As they walked through the streets, Dr. Kalley heard the violent cries. "Death to the wolf from Scotland!"

The plan worked. The men carried Dr. Kalley safely on board. His wife Margaret joined him. They were safe at last. But all their belongings were gone. Their house had been burned down. It seemed that all was lost. But it was not so! Even though the Kalleys had to leave, the church on Madeira kept growing. The Bible took root in the hearts of many. God's Word is powerful. Some believers stayed on Madeira. Other Christians went to the United States for safety.

MISSION TO BRAZIL

In Him [Jesus] was life, and the life was the light of men. And the light shines in the darkness, and the darkness did not comprehend it. (John 1:4-5)

After the Madeira mission, Dr. Kalley and his wife traveled to many places. Margaret's health was still weak. For a time, the couple stayed in Lebanon. The weather there was mild, like Madeira.

Rio de Janeiro in the early 1800s

But in God's providence, Margaret Kalley went to be with her Lord. This happened in 1851. Dr. Kalley grieved the loss of his beloved wife. He stayed in Lebanon for a year.

While there, he met a woman named Sarah Wilson. They became friends. Then, in 1852, they married. Sarah was enthusiastic about her new husband's gospel work. They prayed about where to go next. In 1855, they boarded a ship for Brazil. Dr. Kalley wrote, "I am going to Brazil to bring God's Word of peace. It is my hope that eternal fruit will come of this. This mission is worth laboring for. It is worth suffering for. It is even worth dying for."

In May 1855, the ship *Great Western* dropped anchor in Rio de Janeiro. The bay of Rio was gorgeous. But the Kalleys were not impressed with the city. Trash and sewage filled the streets. Many people in the city lived in broken-down shacks. Disease and death killed many. It was not a pleasant place to be.

Dr. Kalley asked Sarah, "What do you think? Can we stay here?"

"*Ficaremos*," Sarah replied in Portuguese. This word meant, "We will stay."

Dr. Kalley and Sarah would stay in Brazil for twenty-one years.

They now needed a place to live. They moved to a nearby village called Petropolis. There, a number of Germans lived. The Germans were Protestants. They were not part of the Roman Catholic church. Petropolis was a good starting point for Dr. Kalley's mission.

Dr. Kalley was good at speaking with people. He knew how to strike up a conversation. Within minutes, he could find a way to talk about the gospel to someone he met.

Mrs. Kalley explained her husband's gift. "My husband was very gifted at talking to people. He could speak with anyone. It didn't matter what type of person it was. He knew the right things to say. I often timed him. Within three minutes of meeting someone, he talked about spiritual things. People were often surprised by how he did this. But that didn't stop my dear husband. He spoke directly to others about our Lord."

Dr. Kalley held family worship in his home each day. He and his wife invited others to join them. Many locals learned about the Bible through this time of worship. Dr. Kalley told them, "Invite your friends and neighbors! Together, we will sing hymns. We will read the Bible and pray."

Petrópolis, Brazil

Dr. Robert Kalley serving the sick

At times, plagues swept through Brazil. During such times, Dr. Kalley went into action. His skills as a doctor were put to good use. As in Madeira, he always prayed with his patients. He read the Bible to them.

A church was soon started in Petropolis. Not long after, other churches sprang up in nearby cities. Dr. Kalley trained the people of Brazil to help others. He trained them to be teachers of the Bible as well.

THE CHURCH GROWS

Then the churches throughout all Judea, Galilee, and Samaria had peace and were edified. And walking in the fear of the Lord and in the comfort of the Holy Spirit, they were multiplied. (Acts 9:31)

But trouble came to Dr. Kalley's work in Brazil as well. Soon persecution came upon the young church.

One man named Vianna suffered much. He was a **colporteur**. He carried Bibles and other books about God through the streets. He would give these books to anyone who wanted one. But people often attacked him. They threw rocks at him. They hurled insults. Sometimes, someone would steal his bag of books and then scatter them in the streets.

Colporteur (pronounced "cole-porter")

A person who travels and gives away Bibles and other Christian books.

This didn't stop Vianna. It only made him more eager to share God's Word with others.

In Rio de Janeiro, a shop owner named Bernardino came to know Christ. Through reading the Bible, he was saved. Soon his kitchen became a gathering place for Bible study. One evening, a few families gathered at Bernardino's for study and prayer. Later on, there was a knock on the door. Some policemen barged into Bernardino's kitchen. They arrested all the men at the Bible study. Then they began to arrest the women and children.

But Bernardino urged them to stop. He said, "Please, sirs, I beg you! Do not take the women and children. They have done nothing wrong. Please, arrest only us men." The police agreed. The women and children were left alone.

The next day, the police tried to make the men agree not to hold any more Bible studies. "Sign this document," they said. "You must promise that there will be no more house meetings. If you agree, we will release you immediately."

But Bernardino and the other men refused. "We cannot agree to this. We must be able to meet to worship God. If we have to remain in prison or sign this, then we will remain in prison."

One of the brothers, a man named Pitt, visited the men in prison. He was amazed by their joy and courage. Pitt returned to the church and reported. "Our brothers are rejoicing to suffer for Christ! Let us pray for their release."

Emperor Pedro II (1825-1891)

The church gathered for prayer. They asked God to set the men free. While they were praying, the authorities decided to release the men. God answered their prayers. The church in Rio continued to grow and multiply.

Robert and Sarah Kalley kept very busy. Dr. Kalley toured Brazil. Wherever he went, he preached and taught. He trained the men of Brazil to become pastors. He also created a hymnbook. It is still used today. The book was called *Psalmos e Hinos* (Psalms and Hymns). Dr. Kalley also spoke to the government of Brazil. He asked them to allow Christians to live and worship in the country. He became friends with Emperor Pedro II. Pedro was the ruler of Brazil.

Through Dr. Kalley, God did great things in Brazil. People were saved from their sins. The churches grew and grew. Bibles were read. Religious freedom increased. Sick people were healed.

After twenty-one years of labor, Dr. and Mrs. Kalley returned to Scotland. The year was 1876. Dr. Kalley was no longer in Brazil. But that did not mean his work was finished. He continued to help missions in other lands. He wrote letters to the churches in Brazil as well.

In 1888, he fell asleep in Jesus. But he left behind a legacy. There are hundreds of churches in Brazil today influenced by Dr. Kalley. His work ended. But Jesus' work continues in Brazil today.

BASIC FACTS ABOUT BRAZIL

FEDERATIVE REPUBLIC OF BRAZIL	
Total population:	210 million
Total area:	3.3 million square miles
Capital:	Brasília
Official language:	Portuguese
Primary religion:	Roman Catholic

PRAYER POINTS: BRAZIL

Now, take some time to pray for the people of Brazil.

- **Thank God for Brazilians Who Follow Christ**
  The Lord Jesus came to seek and save the lost. That is what Jesus has done for many in Brazil. Give thanks to God for many followers of Jesus in Brazil.

- **Pray for Workers in Far-Away Regions**
  Brazil is a big country. There are many unreached people in it. Many who live in the forests and mountains have never heard the gospel. Ask the Lord to send the light of Christ there.

- **Pray for Christians to Share Christ**
  Pray that many Christians would share their faith with others. Ask God to use their witness to save others.

Toucan

Lapacho trees in Paraguay

20 W.B. GRUBB: THE PARAGUAYAN CHACO

One lone canoe silently made its way up the Paraguay River. Aboard the small craft was Wilfrid Barbrooke Grubb. Mr. Grubb was a missionary from England.

Mr. Grubb was British. But he had left his home and moved to Paraguay for one reason: he wanted to reach the native tribes of the Chaco.

The journey had not been easy. Traveling by canoe was no luxury cruise. Mr. Grubb's boots were muddy. His clothes were dirty. Insects buzzed around his head constantly. The heat was sweltering. On some days, it reached 110°.

Mr. Grubb steered his canoe towards the bank. As he was about to set foot on land, he heard a loud thud. Something had struck the side of the canoe. Mr. Grubb looked down.

Just inches from his feet lay an alligator. The alligator's mouth was wide open. It was ready to crunch the canoe. After the canoe, Mr. Grubb's feet would be next.

Mr. Grubb moved swiftly. Grabbing the canoe paddle, he thrust it into the alligator's mouth. But the paddle was no match for the creature's strong snout and sharp teeth. The alligator snapped it in half like cheap wood.

Seeing that the paddle would not stop the beast, Mr. Grubb grabbed a shovel. He forced the head of the shovel into the alligator's mouth. The iron shovel was not easily crunched. Then he jumped onto the bank, took out his axe, and killed the alligator.

Alligator meat was not Mr. Grubb's planned dinner. But now it was on the menu. He gladly shared the meat with some of the Chaco natives. The natives were excited for a free meal.

Such were some of the perils of the Chaco wilderness. Mr. Grubb left all the comforts of England behind when he came here. He traded those comforts for the dangers of the Chaco.

Why did he do it?

He did it because the natives of the Chaco needed Christ just like Mr. Grubb did.

South American Caiman

THE CHACO REGION

Flat. Hot. Muddy. Those three words describe the Gran Chaco.

In the heart of South America lies the Gran Chaco. It is a large flat-land region. While it is dry, it is not a desert. There are many forests in the Chaco. But the forests are not as dense as rainforests.

Nine months out of the year, much of the Chaco becomes a vast swamp. Rain fills the flat lands. This creates one very big mud pit.

As you might imagine, such swampy conditions invite many insects. Some of the flies that live in the Chaco can grow to be an inch long. Mosquitoes abound.

Today, few people live in this part of Paraguay. But for thousands of years, native people groups made the Chaco their home.

Today, cattle ranching and farming are common there. But there still aren't many roads. There were even fewer roads a hundred years ago.

In 1890, when Mr. Grubb entered the Chaco, travel was even more difficult. Mr. Grubb found this to be a wild, hard land. But it wasn't just tough wilderness he had to deal with. He also had to deal with tough, dry, rocky hearts. Mr. Grubb shared the faith with the Chaco Indians.

Cattle on the Chaco

CONFRONTING CHACO WITCH DOCTORS

Inasmuch then as the children have partaken of flesh and blood, He [Jesus] Himself likewise shared in the same, that through death He might destroy him who had the power of death, that is, the devil, and release those who through fear of death were all their lifetime subject to bondage. (Hebrews 2:14-15)

Starting in 1890, Mr. Grubb built mission stations in the Chaco. Sometimes the Indians welcomed him. They could see that he loved them. Many realized that he had come to help them. But the witch doctors of the Chaco tribes felt differently about him. They didn't like him at all. They knew that God was with him. They knew Mr. Grubb brought a power that was stronger than theirs. This power would destroy their authority over the natives.

Witch doctors held great power over the native tribes. They ruled over the tribes because the people were afraid of them. They used magic spells and claimed to have power over evil spirits. The Chaco Indians lived in constant fear. They believed that evil spirits were everywhere. If these spirits got angry, they might kill animals or destroy gardens. The Chaco believed they had to keep the spirits happy. If they didn't, famine or death would come upon them.

How did the Indians keep the spirits happy? They brought gifts to the witch doctor. The witch doctor told them that these gifts would make angry spirits happy.

But who really gained anything from the gifts? It was the witch doctors.

Mr. Grubb taught a different faith. He taught the Chaco about the one true God. He told them about Jesus, the Savior of the world. He said that Jesus would set them free from the bondage of evil spirits.

One day Mr. Grubb set out on a journey. He loaded his ox cart with sup-
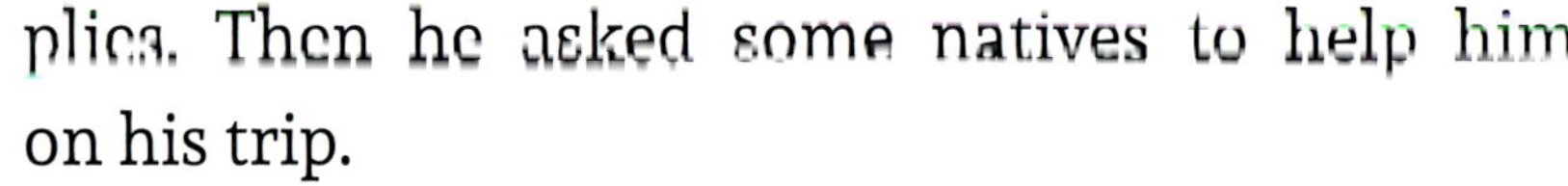
plies. Then he asked some natives to help him on his trip.

Wilfrid Barbrooke Grubb (1865-1930)

The witch doctors threatened the natives, "If you help him, we will send the spirits after you. They will bring sickness to your home!"

The natives were afraid. Mr. Grubb would have to make his journey alone. This would not be easy. Pulling an ox cart through the swamps of the Chaco was difficult.

The witch doctors boasted, "Our spells will stop Grubb. He'll never finish his journey. He will die before he gets there."

But they were wrong. Mr. Grubb made the journey without any trouble.

A WRONG BELIEF MIGHT KILL YOU

The natives of the Chaco believed many wrong things about the world. They believed evil spirits controlled the world. They also had strange beliefs about dreams. The Chaco believed that what they dreamed would come true. One day, this wrong belief got Mr. Grubb into terrible trouble.

On December 13, 1897, Mr. Grubb was taking a journey with a Chaco named Po-wit.

Mr. Grubb trusted Po-wit. They had often spent time together. But that

Illustration of W.B. Grubb in the Chaco

morning, Po-wit would betray him.

As they walked through the forest, Mr. Grubb snapped branches so he could get through the trees. Po-wit followed closely behind him.

For a moment, Mr. Grubb knelt down. As he kneeled, he heard a "twang." Then he felt an arrow pierce his back. The arrowhead lodged in one of his ribs.

Po-wit had shot Mr. Grubb. But Mr. Grubb didn't know it. He cried out for help. "Po-wit, come help me! I've been shot!"

Po-wit shouted, "Oh, Mr. Grubb! Mr. Grubb!" Then he ran into the forest. Mr. Grubb was left alone.

Mr. Grubb was in much pain. But he was able to move. By God's providence, the arrow had not pierced his lungs.

He removed the arrow with some difficulty. Retracing his steps, he found that Po-wit had stolen all his belongings.

For the next eight days, Mr. Grubb journeyed slowly to the mission station. The pain from the arrow wound was intense. Yet he survived. He arrived

Gran Chaco landscape

at the mission station with little food and a life-threatening wound.

Mr. Grubb spent two weeks in the hospital as he recovered from his wound. Then he was ready to get back to work. After recovering, he learned why Po-wit attacked him.

Many of the Chaco held a false belief about dreams. They believed that a dream told them something that would actually happen. Po-wit dreamed that Mr. Grubb would attack him. So he decided to attack Mr. Grubb first.

False beliefs have consequences. Mr. Grubb learned this very well after Po-wit's attack.

If you had been shot in the back, what would you have done? Would you keep on serving the Chaco? Or would you want to give up and go home?

Surely, it would have been easier to just go home. But Mr. Grubb didn't do that. In love, he continued to serve the Chaco.

JESUS SAVES THE CHACO

"The Son of Man has come to seek and to save that which was lost." (Luke 19:10)

Chacoan peccary

Mr. Grubb knew that missionary work was hard. He spent years talking to the natives about Christ. But many years passed without a single Chaco trusting in Jesus.

Mr. Grubb wrote, "It may be years before any Chaco believe in Jesus. We leave this to God. Only the Holy Spirit can change hearts. We are only required to be faithful. God doesn't reward us because we save many souls. He gives His reward to faithful servants."

In 1899, two people got saved and were baptized. This was just the beginning. In the years that followed, some whole villages became Christian. The church grew more each year.

Mr. Grubb continued faithfully for many years. He lived in South America until 1921. Then he returned to Great Britain. But even in his last years, his work did not end. In England and Scotland, he kept praying for the Chaco. He urged others to support the work in Paraguay.

Cerro Paraguari mountains

Was the sacrifice worth it? Was it worth it to endure mud, scorching heat, alligators, arrows, and more?

Yes, it was worth it. Mr. Grubb's labors were not in vain.

Therefore, my beloved brethren, be steadfast, immovable, always abounding in the work of the Lord, knowing that your labor is not in vain in the Lord. (1 Corinthians 15:58)

BASIC FACTS ABOUT PARAGUAY

REPUBLIC OF PARAGUAY	
Total population:	7 million
Total area:	158,000 square miles
Capital:	Asunción
Official language:	Spanish
Primary religion:	Roman Catholic

PRAYER POINTS: PARAGUAY

Now, take some time to pray for the people of Paraguay.

- **Pray for Wise Leaders who Fear God**
  Paraguay has suffered through many wars. Sometimes, the nation has been ruled by unwise leaders. Pray that God would send righteous leaders. Pray for leaders who fear God. Pray that many faithful Christians would serve in the government.
- **Give Thanks to God for the Growth of the Church**
  Give thanks to God. There was a time when no people in Paraguay worshiped the one true God. Now, many worship the Lord. Praise God for His mercy to the peoples of Paraguay.
- **Pray for Christian Education**
  Many children in Paraguay do not go to school. Many have to work all the time to help provide for their families. Ask the Lord to give godly teachers to these children in Paraguay. Ask God to send faithful men and women who will teach God's Word to these people.

21

DWIGHT L. MOODY: AMERICAN EVANGELIST

A loud *rap-rap-rap* was heard at the front door. Slowly young Dwight creaked the door open and looked up.

Standing at the door was Mr. Ezra Purple. Dwight knew why Mr. Purple was there. He had come to get the money he was owed.

Mr. Purple spoke first. “Boy, is your mother home?”

“Yes, sir,” Dwight replied. “But she’s in bed. She is still recovering from having a baby.”

“I must see her right away.”

Mr. Purple pushed his way inside past Dwight. With an angry scowl on his face, he entered Mrs. Moody’s bedroom.

“Betsy, I’ve come to collect the money I am owed.”

Mrs. Betsy Moody looked up in surprise. Here she was in bed, resting and caring for her newborn twins. She watched in shock as Mr. Purple barged into her bedroom.

“I’m sorry, Mr. Purple. I don’t have the money to pay you right now. As you know, my husband just passed away, and I have to feed and care for my nine children. Would you be patient with us? I will pay you as soon as I can.”

Mr. Purple shouted a few mean words at Betsy. Then he stormed out of the house.

The Moody family was poor. Dwight’s father had died from a heart attack. Betsy could barely afford to feed her children. Life was difficult.

Dwight asked his mother, “Mom, how will we pay the bills? We only have a little bread left. What is going to happen to us?”

“My son, we must trust in the Lord. He is a good Father. He knows what we need. The Lord shall provide.”

Betsy Moody was right. The Lord did provide. In Northfield, Massachusetts lived a pastor. His name was Oliver Everett, and he was a godly man. Pastor Everett decided to bring food to the Moody home. He also taught the children how to read and write.

Dwight and his brothers and sisters learned about God. Dwight's mother and pastor both trusted in the Lord. This was a good example for young Dwight.

The Bible says that true religion is to visit orphans and widows and care for them (James 1:27). Pastor Everett obeyed this verse.

DWIGHT GROWS UP

When my father and my mother forsake me,
Then the Lord will take care of me. (Psalm 27:10)

Dwight started earning money when he was just a boy. When he was ten years old, he went to Greenfield, Massachusetts to work.

After work one day, an old man passed Dwight in the street. The man's hair was white, and he walked slowly with a cane.

"Young man, tell me your name," the old man said.

"My name is Dwight, sir," Dwight replied.

The man then asked, "Where are you from? Who is your father?"

"I live in Northfield, sir. My father's name was Edwin. He died when I was young, sir."

The old man was touched by Dwight's sad situation. He stretched out his hand and placed it on the boy's head.

"Young man, I am sad to hear that your father has died. You may not have an earthly father now. But know that you have a Heavenly Father. He loves you very much."

The man gave Dwight some money as a blessing. Dwight never forgot the old man's words.

These early memories stuck with Dwight. But as he grew older, he became friends with ungodly young men. He began to join in the sinful ways of these young men. He took God's name in vain and often got into fights with other boys. He was a proud young man. He was not yet humbled.

DWIGHT BELIEVES IN JESUS CHRIST

"Believe on the Lord Jesus Christ, and you will be saved, you and your household." (Acts 16:31)

Plaque in Boston commemorating Dwight Moody's conversion

When Dwight was seventeen, he moved to Boston. His mother didn't want him to go, but he went anyway.

Dwight's uncle Samuel lived in Boston. He owned a shoe store. Dwight visited Uncle Samuel and asked for a job.

"Uncle, will you let me work here? I need money if I am to stay in Boston."

Samuel hesitated. He knew Dwight was a proud young man. It is hard to work with proud young men. They are not teachable.

After thinking on it, Samuel decided to offer Dwight a job.

"Very well, Dwight. You may work here. However, there are some rules you must follow. First off, you must obey my instructions. And you have to attend church with me each Sunday."

Dwight L. Moody (1837-1899)

Dwight agreed to the rules.

Each Sunday, Dwight went with Uncle Samuel to Mt. Vernon Congregational Church. He found it quite boring. Sometimes he fell asleep during the service. After church had ended, he couldn't remember what the sermon had been about.

But Dwight did enjoy one thing about church. He liked his Sunday school teacher. His teacher's name was Edward Kimball.

Mr. Kimball cared about Dwight. He knew that this young man had not submitted his life to Jesus. Mr. Kimball thought to himself, "It is time for me to confront Dwight. He needs to believe in Jesus."

One morning, Mr. Kimball visited the shoe store. He found Dwight stocking shelves in the back room.

"Hello, Mr. Kimball!" Dwight said.

Mr. Kimball had tears in his eyes. He began to speak.

"Dwight, it is good to see you, my boy! I wanted to tell you something very important. You have been in my Sunday school class for some time. But I don't think you are following Jesus. Dwight, I want you to know that Jesus Christ loves you. He calls you to repent of your sins and to trust in Him. Jesus calls you to love Him. Will you commit your life to follow Jesus?"

Dwight was moved by Mr. Kimball's words. He knew from these words and the man's tears that Mr. Kimball loved him. God used this love in a powerful way. Right then, Dwight turned from his life of sin and pride and confessed that Jesus was his Lord and Savior. That day, he began to live a different life. The year was 1856.

DWIGHT BECOMES AN EVANGELIST

Dwight's love for Christ grew every day. He loved to read the Bible. He found delight in prayer. He also wanted to share the good news of Jesus with others.

In 1856, he moved to Chicago. He found good opportunities for work here. But he also found good opportunities for **evangelism**.

Evangelism

To share the truth of Jesus' gospel with other people. Evangelists urge others to believe in Jesus and be saved from their sins.

Inspired by Mr. Kimball, Dwight started his own Sunday school. He found homeless or wandering boys on the streets of Chicago and invited them to Sunday school. Dwight knew what it was like to be poor and without a father. He taught the boys about Jesus' love for the world.

Moody's first Sunday school

Dwight was gifted in evangelism. Soon, his Sunday school grew to have over 1500 children! Dwight also started a church in Chicago in 1864.

Many people in Chicago came to hear him preach. They loved his simple Bible teaching. Before long, people all over Chicago knew who Dwight Moody was.

THE GREAT FIRE OF 1871

If a trumpet is blown in a city, will not the people be afraid?
If there is calamity in a city, will not the LORD have done it? (Amos 3:6)

Disaster struck Chicago on October 8, 1871. A small fire started in a farm near the city. What started small grew to be very large. Soon, the fire spread across Chicago.

That night, Dwight preached to thousands. In a large hall in Chicago, he called sinners to faith and repentance.

Great Fire of Chicago, 1871

People sitting in the pews wondered, "How long will he go on preaching? There's a fire outside!"

The clanging fire bells could be heard outside. Dwight preached on.

"Consider the claims of Jesus Christ. Who is He? Who do you say that He is? The Bible says He is the Savior of the world!"

The roar of fire engines continued outside. Dwight preached on.

Finally, the service ended. People rushed home. Dwight and his family also returned to their house. The flames drew near to the Moody home.

Quickly, Dwight, his wife Emma, and his children grabbed their valuables and fled the house. Soon it was engulfed in flames.

By God's mercy, the Moody family was safe. However, 17,000 buildings burned in Chicago. Over 300 people died. Dwight's gospel message was urgent that night. He knew that this might be the last time many ever heard the gospel.

PREACHING OVERSEAS

Across the Atlantic Ocean lived an older woman named Marianne Adlard. She lived in London, England. Due to illness, she was confined to her bed.

Marianne felt like she could not do much for the Lord. But she could pray. So that is what she did every day.

Each day, Marianne prayed that God's Spirit would revive the churches. She prayed, "Lord, would You send Your Spirit to us? Please build Your church. Save many souls."

One day, Marianne heard about Dwight's work in Chicago. She heard how the Lord was using him to share the gospel. Many in America had been saved. She prayed, "Lord, would You send us this man? Send him to our church to preach!"

Dwight didn't know anything about Marianne or her prayers. But the Lord heard Marianne.

In 1872, the Moody family decided to visit England. Dwight didn't plan to preach though. He traveled overseas to meet other pastors.

English pastors heard Dwight was visiting. They sent him letters, asking, "Mr. Moody, will you preach at our church?"

A man named Pastor Lessey invited Dwight to preach at his church in London. Dwight agreed and preached twice on Sunday. The people were hungry for God's Word. Many talked to Dwight and Pastor Lessey afterwards. They were anxious about the state of their souls. They wanted to be right with God.

Dwight Moody preaching

Dwight then took a trip to Ireland. But after arriving, he got a message from Pastor Lessey.

Mr. Moody, would you return to London? My people would like to hear you preach more. There is a hunger for God here. Please come again as soon as you can. – Pastor John Lessey

---

Dwight returned to London. Then, for ten days, he preached every day. Over 400 people put their faith in Christ. Dwight and Pastor Lessey were amazed by God's saving power!

While there, Dwight learned about Marianne Adlard. Pastor Lessey told him, "Brother Moody, she has been praying that you would come to England."

Dwight exclaimed, "Well, I do believe God has heard her! He brought me over 4,000 miles across land and sea to answer her request."

SCHOOLS FOR GIRLS AND BOYS

In 1876, Dwight returned to his hometown of Northfield. He had compassion on the poor children living there. He knew how hard it was to be poor and orphaned. Dwight decided to build a school for girls and a school for boys. First, he started Northfield Seminary. This was a school for girls. Then he opened Mount Hermon Boys School.

Northfield Mount Hermon School

In God's providence, Mount Hermon Boys School was built on Ezra Purple's old farm! It was the same farm where Dwight grew up as a boy.

Before building, Dwight took a few friends to the farm. There they prayed for God's blessing to be on the school. Dwight told the people with him:

My friends, it was on this very farm that I grew up as a boy. After my father died, we barely had food and clothing. Old Man Purple was very harsh. He demanded his mortgage payments. But my mother could not pay. When I started making more money, I planned to buy this farm one day. But thanks be to God! Now I am glad that I don't own this farm. Instead, I lay this farm at the feet of my Savior Jesus. Here we will build a school. It will be a school for boys like me. Here we will teach boys the Bible.

LAST YEARS

For the rest of his life, Dwight kept on preaching about Christ. He traveled throughout America. In 1899, he preached his last sermon. It was a sermon about heaven.

We call this earth the "land of the living?" I tell you, it is not. This is the land of the dying. What is our life here? It is a vapor. But look at the next world. No death. No pain. No sorrow. No old age. No sickness. No tears. Instead, in heaven, there is joy, peace, and love. Think of it! Life without end! Yet so many choose life on this earth. Don't close your heart. Take the gift of eternal life!

Before he died, Dwight said, "I have been looking forward to this day for years!"

On December 22, 1899, Dwight went to be with Jesus. The poor boy from Northfield was used mightily by the Lord.

Lapwai, Idaho

HENRY AND ELIZA SPALDING: AMONG THE NEZ PERCE

22

"Look to Me, and be saved,
All you ends of the earth!
For I am God, and there is no other." (Isaiah 45:22)

In 1805, American explorers Lewis and Clark made their way across America. That year, they met a tribe called the Nez Perce. The Nez Perce lived in the Pacific Northwest. This part of the United States includes Idaho, Oregon, and Washington. It is believed that the Nez Perce first heard about the Bible from Lewis and Clark.

Thirty years later, the first missionaries were sent to the Pacific Northwest. Two couples served in this wild land. Marcus and Narcissa Whitman worked among the Cayuse Indians. Henry and Eliza Spalding served the Nez Perce. These two couples set up mission stations about one hundred miles apart.

In the early 1800s, this land was wilderness. Few roads existed. There were no trains. Travel was slow and difficult. Many Indian tribes lived here. Some of the tribes were dangerous. The Spaldings and Whitmans went west by faith. They trusted God for daily bread and for safety.

THE NEZ PERCE MISSION

Henry and his wife Eliza lived in Lapwai. Today, this land is part of the state of Idaho. Henry and Eliza worked hard to learn the language of these people.

Henry H. Spalding
(1803-1874)

Many tribes relied on buffalo meat for food. But with so much hunting, the buffalo herds were getting smaller and smaller. Each year, it was harder to find food. Henry taught the Indians how to grow their own food. He started a ranch. He also brought the first potato crop to Idaho. Now, Idaho is called the potato capital of the world. The Spaldings built a flour mill and a sawmill. Cattle, sheep, and hogs were raised. They taught the Indians to work and to be productive.

A printing press was shipped to Lapwai. Henry and Eliza used this to print books for the natives. They began to translate the Bible and hymns. Henry also preached to the Indians. Sometimes, over 2,000 Indians came to the services. The Lord used Henry to save many Indians. Soon, natives came to be baptized. They confessed the name of Jesus Christ. Henry and Eliza were filled with joy.

Eliza opened a school in Lapwai. She was a gifted teacher. She taught the Nez Perce how to read and write their own language. When she and her husband began printing books, the natives could read them. The first book they printed was a hymnbook. The Spaldings taught the Indians to sing praises to God.

Nez Perce women admired Eliza. They followed her around the

Henry Spalding with his printing press

ranch. From her they learned many helpful skills. They learned how to be godly women too.

The Lapwai settlement kept growing. By 1847, it had grown large indeed. It had forty-four acres of land used for farming. Over a hundred animals lived on the land. There were two schools, a church meetinghouse, and a blacksmith shop. There was also a granary where food was stored.

God also blessed the Spaldings with four children. Their names were Eliza, Henry, Martha, and Amelia. Eliza, born in 1837, was the first white American girl born in Idaho. All four children were born at the Lapwai mission.

This was the beginning of the Nez Perce Mission.

THE WHITMAN MASSACRE

My brethren, count it all joy when you fall into various trials, knowing that the testing of your faith produces patience. (James 1:2-3)

The Lord blessed the Nez Perce mission. Henry and Eliza's ministry bore fruit. But in 1847, trouble came.

Their daughter Eliza went to school at the Whitman mission one hundred miles away. She was ten years old in November 1847. In that month, tragedy

Depiction of the Whitman massacre

struck the Whitman mission. The Cayuse Indians attacked. They murdered all the men and some of the women. Then they took the rest of the women and children hostage. Eliza was one of these. She and fifty other women and children were taken hostage. They were kept as captives for a month. During this time, some of the women and children died.

When other settlers heard what had happened, they came to help. They tried to rescue the women and children from the Indians. The Indians asked for a ransom. After this was paid, they let the captives go free. Eliza returned home. Henry and mother Eliza were relieved. Their prayers for her safety had been answered.

After the massacre, the people in charge of the Nez Perce mission began to wonder. Would the Nez Perce also attack? They were concerned about the Spaldings. They told Henry and Eliza to leave Lapwai. Henry and Eliza obeyed. But they were heartbroken. What would happen to the Indian Christians? Who would teach them? Would the worship of God continue?

The Spaldings didn't know what would happen. They packed their things and moved to Oregon. They settled in a town called Brownsville. There they opened a school and started a church. Henry became the pastor. He taught God's people in Brownsville from 1847 to 1859.

In 1851, Henry faced one of the hardest days of his life. His wife Eliza died. She was forty-three years old. This was a very sad time. Later, the Lord would send a new wife for Henry. Her name was Rachel. All this time, Henry was praying. He kept asking God to let him return to the Nez Perce. His heart was with the Indians at Lapwai.

RETURN TO THE NEZ PERCE

Trust in the Lord with all your heart,
And lean not on your own understanding;
In all your ways acknowledge Him,
And He shall direct your paths. (Proverbs 3:5-6)

God opened the door in 1865. Henry returned to Lapwai to take up the mission. When he arrived, he heard very good news. About 1,000 of the Indians had kept the faith. Henry was gone almost twenty years. During that time, the Christian Indians continued to follow Jesus. Henry thanked God for this. Then he began preaching to them again. With joy, the Christian Nez Perce received back their old pastor.

Home at Fort Lapwai

Alice Lake, Idaho

Sadly, Henry's return did not last long. Some men in the government decided to replace him. They sent someone else to Lapwai, and Henry had to leave. That same year, he left a second time and returned to Brownsville.

All this time, Henry had been working on the Bible. He had translated the Gospel of Matthew into the Nez Perce language. In 1870, he went east. He returned to his home in New York. He spoke with his friends and family and told them about his work. He also visited the American Bible Society. Henry convinced them to print 1,000 copies of his Gospel of Matthew. He would take these copies back to the Nez Perce.

Henry also talked to the United States Congress in 1871. They wanted to know about the Nez Perce. They wanted to know how they could help them. Henry told them about the Indians. He shared his ideas with Congress. Then he was allowed to return to Lapwai. Once again, he preached God's Word to the people. He also translated the Book of Acts into Nez Perce.

By the end of Henry's time in Lapwai, over 1,200 Indians came to know Christ. But in 1874, Henry's work came to an end. On August 3, 1874, he departed and went to be with Christ.

The Lord Jesus brought His salvation to the Nez Perce. Those thousands of Indians in Christ now sing His praises! Thanks be to God!

BASIC FACTS ABOUT THE NEZ PERCE TRIBE OF IDAHO

NEZ PERCE INDIAN RESERVATION	
Total population:	3,500
Total area:	1,200 square miles
Headquarters:	Lapwai, Idaho
Languages:	English, Nez Perce
Primary religion:	Roman Catholic

PRAYER POINTS: NEZ PERCE TRIBE

Now, take some time to pray for the Nez Perce.

Today, the Nez Perce people still live in Idaho. There are about 3,500 members of the tribe. They live on a large piece of land called a reservation. This is a special piece of land set aside for the Indians to live on. The Nez Perce still speak their own language. They have two major salmon hatcheries on their land. These are places where salmon are hatched. After they hatch, the little fish are released into the wild. This helps to build the salmon population.

Some Nez Perce still follow Christ. But others follow their old tribal religion. There are a number of churches on the reservation. One of these still sings hymns in the Nez Perce language. It is a Presbyterian church.

- **Praise God for Christian Faith among the Nez Perce**
  Praise the Lord for what He has done among the Nez Perce. Many of these Indians believe in Christ. In the past and in the present, many believe in Jesus as Lord.
- **Pray for the Nez Perce Nation**
  The Nez Perce are a small people group today. Pray that they would all turn to the Lord Jesus.

Brown bears fishing in Alaska

A LIGHT IN THE NORTH: CLAH BRINGS THE GOSPEL TO ALASKA

23

I will bring the blind by a way they did not know;
I will lead them in paths they have not known.
I will make darkness light before them,
And crooked places straight.
These things I will do for them,
And not forsake them. (Isaiah 42:16)

Far to the north, on the western coast of Canada, is a little village called Fort Simpson. Fort Simpson is very close to Alaska. This little village lies on the shore of the Pacific Ocean. High mountains covered with snow rise behind it. For many months out of the year, Fort Simpson is covered in snow too. Here in this cold village, a child was born about the year 1848. His name was Clah.

Many Indian tribes lived near Fort Simpson. Clah was part of the Tsimshian tribe. His full name was Wil-um-clah. This name means "an eagle swooping down and capturing its prey." Clah's parents gave him this name because they hoped he would become a mighty and brave warrior.

When Clah was a little boy, his father started training him to be a strong man. His father said, "My son will become strong by doing hard things." When winter came, Clah's father and the men in the village picked up long sticks. With these sticks, they chased Clah and other boys into the water of the ocean. Snow covered the ground, and the water was ice-cold. The boys almost froze to death.

"This will make my son strong!" Clah's father cried.

As Clah grew, his father taught him many things. He learned to do very wicked deeds with the other Indians. These Indian tribes lived in terrible sin. Their villages were filled with murder and wickedness. They sold their daughters as slaves. Some of the Indians were **cannibals**. A cannibal is someone who eats other people. Clah learned all these things while he was still a boy.

GOD SAVES A WICKED MAN

So Jesus had compassion and touched their eyes. And immediately their eyes received sight, and they followed Him. (Matthew 20:34)

When Clah became a young man, he went to a British town in Canada to start earning money. While he was there, he heard someone preaching about Jesus. Clah had never heard of Jesus, so he listened to the man talk. But when the sermon was over, Clah shook his head and walked away. He wasn't interested in the gospel.

Later on, Clah got into trouble. He was a violent young man, and he did many wicked things. Because of this, the British arrested him and put him in jail. When Clah was released from jail, he got in a canoe and went home to Fort Simpson.

Frontier town in the 1800s

Clah had heard the truth about Jesus and didn't listen to it, but God wasn't finished yet. When Clah reached his home village, he found out that it had changed. Some Christian Indians had come there. They were teaching the people the same thing that Clah had heard about Jesus. God began to work in Clah's heart, and he became a Christian. His wife became a Christian too. In 1873, they were baptized.

Now Clah knew that the wicked things he had learned as a boy were very wrong. He didn't want to be like the Indians anymore. He decided to choose a new name to show that he had a new life in Jesus. His new name was Philip McKay.

Clah was filled with joy when he learned about God. He wanted to know more, so he began to learn English so he could read the Bible. He began to memorize the Bible too.

Totem poles in Wrangell

AN ARMY CAPTAIN AND A CHURCH

Blessed is the Lord God of Israel, for He has visited and redeemed His people. (Luke 1:68)

In 1876, Clah went to Alaska to find work. Many people from the United States had come to Alaska. They came to work or to look for gold. Clah got a job cutting firewood. He worked for some men in the American army at Fort Wrangell.

Clah worked hard for six days every week. But when Sunday came, he and some Christian Indians stopped working. They gathered together to worship God.

One of the men from the army saw Clah stop working. His name was Captain Jocelyn.

"Why aren't you working today?" the captain asked.

"Today is the Lord's Day," Clah replied. "This is a special day for worshiping God."

Captain Jocelyn was surprised to hear this. He knew many Indians, but they were all wicked people. None of them worshiped the true God.

"I didn't know you were a Christian," he said to Clah. Then his face filled with joy. "God is working among the Indians, and I am very glad to see it!"

Clah and the Christian Indians didn't have a church to worship in. But the captain found a building they could use. They didn't have any Bibles either.

"I will find some Bibles for you," the captain said. He got some Bibles and hymnbooks and gave them to Clah. "Use these for your church."

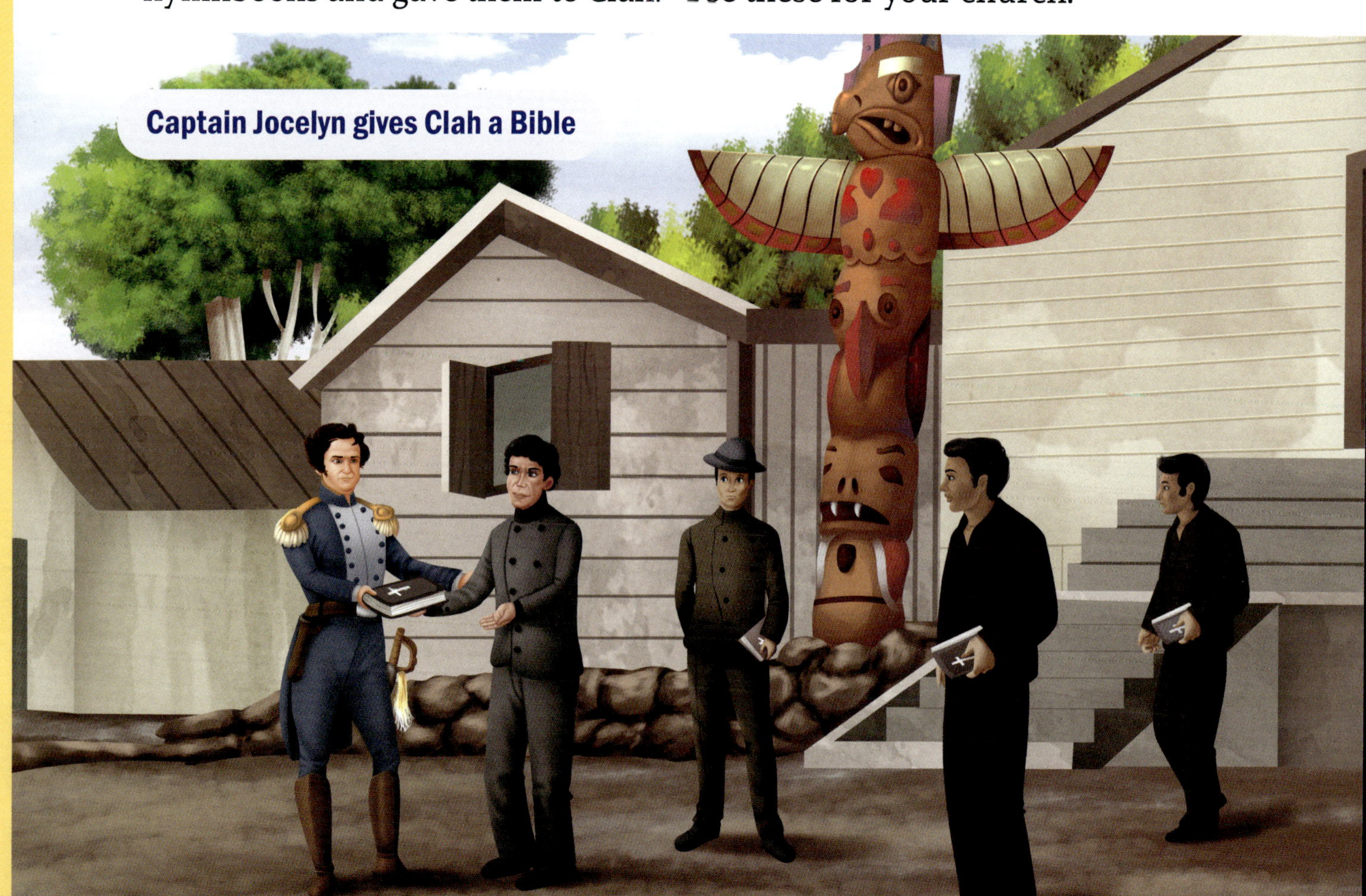
Captain Jocelyn gives Clah a Bible

Clah thankfully took the Bibles. Then he and the Christian Indians gathered in the little building to worship God. Soon other Indians came to see what they were doing. Some came to listen, but others began to mock them. They made fun of Clah as he preached. They caused so much noise that it was hard for the Christians to worship together.

When Captain Jocelyn heard what the other Indians were doing, he sent soldiers to the little building. "Stand by the door so that no one bothers the Christians," he told the soldiers. The guards stood quietly while the church met. When the wicked Indians saw them, they knew they couldn't disturb the Christians anymore.

GOD SAVES THE ALASKAN INDIANS

Many nations shall come and say,
"Come, and let us go . . . to the house of the God of Jacob;
He will teach us His ways,
And we shall walk in His paths." (Micah 4:2)

Many Indians heard about Clah and his little church. They came to listen.

God began to save them, and soon hundreds of Indians started to worship God. They left their wicked ways and turned to the Lord.

"The Lord died for me?" one Indian asked. "I will not be proud anymore. I will not live a life of sin now. I will serve this God who loves me!"

The church became so big that Clah preached three times each Sunday. He preached every night during the week too. He also went to other villages to talk to the Indians. He read God's Word to the people and begged them to listen to it.

"The Indian tribes are afraid of the Bible," he said. "They think a big monster will come out of the book and eat them!" But Clah kept preaching. He knew that God could save these tribes just like God had saved him.

Clah also started teaching the Indians to read. He wanted them to be able to read the Bible for themselves. Every day during the week, men and women and little boys and girls came to learn how to read. Clah taught them all.

Clah spent every day teaching and preaching. He taught over sixty people in the school each day. On Sundays, he preached to hundreds of Indians. But sometimes it was hard for him to preach. He had a sickness called tuberculosis. This made it difficult for him to breathe. But Clah kept working to teach the Indians about Jesus.

"I must not stop, even if I am sick," he said. "Who else will teach them if I don't?" Sadness filled his heart when he thought about his people. They were lost in the darkness of their sin. They needed to hear the truth about Jesus. Clah prayed and asked God to send more people to preach His Word.

Captain Jocelyn also prayed. Other American soldiers did too. They sent letters to pastors in Canada and the United States. "Please come help us," they wrote. "The native tribes in Alaska need to hear God's Word. Clah is teaching them, but he needs help. Will you send us help?"

One of these letters reached a man named Sheldon Jackson. He was a pastor in the United States. In August 1877, he and a woman named Amanda McFarland came to Fort Wrangell to help. When they arrived, they went to the church where Clah was preaching. Inside the wooden building, the room was filled with people. The Indians were singing hymns in their own language. Then Clah stood up and prayed. After he finished, all the Indians prayed the

Lord's Prayer together.

Sheldon Jackson's eyes filled with tears of joy as he saw what God was doing in Alaska. But he couldn't stay long. He had to get back to his church in the United States. He promised Clah that he would try to send another pastor soon. Then he left. Mrs. McFarland stayed to help with the school for the Indians.

A SAD DAY AND A HAPPY END

Break forth into joy, sing together, . . .
For the LORD has comforted His people, . . .
And all the ends of the earth shall see
The salvation of our God. (Isaiah 52:9-10)

Clah was glad to have Mrs. McFarland's help. His sickness was getting worse, so he couldn't teach the Indians as much as he wanted to. Two months later, he became very ill. The Indians ran to get Mrs. McFarland.

"Come quickly!" they cried. "Clah is dying!"

Mrs. McFarland came at once. She found Clah lying on his bed.

"Are you ready to die?" she asked him. Clah was very weak, but he nodded.

"I am not afraid to die," he said. "If God wants me to live, I will live. But if He wants me to die, I will be glad to go to Him." Then his face became very sad. "I wanted to see a pastor come here to teach my people before I died. But I will let God do what He thinks is best."

Red fox in Alaska

Clah hoped he would get well so he could keep preaching. But his sickness continued to get worse. On December 28, 1877, he died.

Clah was only thirty years old when he died. But God had used his short life to bring hundreds of Indians to Christ. God had started a mighty work in Alaska. Even though Clah died, God would still answer his prayers. Many preachers would come to continue the work among the Indian tribes in the north. This work is still going on today! Praise God for His mercy to the people of Alaska!

Caribou near Mt. Denali

Mt. Sneffels, San Juan Mountains, Colorado

GEORGE DARLEY: PASTOR TO PROSPECTORS AND GAMBLERS

24

How beautiful upon the mountains
Are the feet of him who brings good news,
Who proclaims peace,
Who brings glad tidings of good things,
Who proclaims salvation,
Who says to Zion,
"Your God reigns!" (Isaiah 52:7)

It was a frigid morning in the San Juan Mountains. The earliest rays of the sun could be seen in the east. Its light cast purple, pink, and orange colors into the sky. The colors mixed together, creating a dazzling sight of beauty. The cold morning was beginning to get a little warmer. But George could still see his breath in the icy stillness of the sunrise.

Pastor George Darley had snowshoed across the mountains. It was now the fifth day of his journey. Five days and four nights had taken a toll on his strength and on his feet. He was cold, sore, and exhausted.

Fifteen degrees Fahrenheit was not unusual for this time of year. But after five days, George was ready to put his feet up next to a roaring fire.

George's trek had led him on a dangerous route over the mountains. He was traveling from Lake City to Ouray, Colorado, a journey of more than 125 miles. Gold miners sometimes made the same journey he was taking. They knew the difficulties of mountain passes and winter weather. But miners made the journey to find gold. Pastor George did not endure hardship to get gold.

George snowshoed for a different purpose. He traveled 125 miles in the snow so that he could preach the gospel. His mission: bring the good news of Jesus to Ouray.

A CHURCH IN LAKE CITY

Blowing winds. Frigid cold. Blizzards. **Avalanches**. Rocky terrain. These were part of normal life for George.

Avalanche

A large amount of snow and ice falling quickly down a mountainside. Avalanches are very dangerous.

Visitors to Colorado are impressed by its rugged terrain. The soil is hard. George faced more than hard terrain in Colorado. He also had to deal with hard hearts. This was much harder for him than rocky ground.

George Darley (1847-1917)

In the 1870s, tens of thousands of people made the journey to southwest Colorado. This was called "the Great San Juan excitement." Mines were tunneled into the mountains. Men came for gold and silver. Where there was a love of money, other sins followed as well. Gambling, drunkenness, and taking God's name in vain were common in mining towns.

The new residents of Colorado came from the eastern states. Many grew up in Christian homes. But when they went west, they forgot God. George said, "Many think that when they cross the Missouri River, God can no longer see them."

George was a carpenter by trade. He was born in 1847 in Nebraska. His father taught him woodworking. Later, George joined his brother Alexander in Colorado. Alexander was a pastor on the frontier. George wanted to become a pastor too.

Together, they established the First Presbyterian Church in Lake City. The year was 1876. By November, a church building was constructed. George did

Old mining equipment near Silverton, Colorado

much of the building work himself. It was the first Protestant church building on the **Western Slope** of Colorado. The church still stands in Lake City today.

Western Slope

Land in Colorado that is located on the western side of the Rocky Mountain range.

JOURNEY TO SILVERTON

In Spring 1877, the Presbyterian church sent George to a town called Silverton. Today, a drive from Lake City to Silverton might take three hours. It was a much harder trip for George.

On May 17, George saddled his horse. It was May. But in the Rocky Mountains, it snows frequently in May. At 9,000 feet above sea level, George reached Lake San Cristobal.

The wind increased. A massive snowstorm swept in. George kept climbing.

His face was frozen. His fingers were numb.

After an hour, he reached a small cabin. There he stayed with a family overnight. Gus Talbot the mailman was also there.

Colorado mountain mailmen held a challenging job. Gus had seen one hundred avalanches on his mail routes. Gus brought the mail over 12,000-foot mountain peaks on snowshoes.

George thought it would be better if he traveled with the mailman. "Gus, I'm heading to Silverton. Why don't we go together?"

The mailman agreed.

George and Gus set out the next morning. Gus was bringing news from families in the East. George was bringing news from the God of heaven. Gus had forty pounds of letters on his back. George had his Bible and pack.

Lake City Presbyterian Church, Lake City, Colorado

The snowstorms were intense. For three hours, Gus and George wandered in circles. They were lost! But eventually the storms subsided. They found the right path once again.

Finally, by God's mercy, George and Gus reached Silverton. Gus was impressed by George's grit and determination.

Gus exclaimed, "You can travel with George M. Darley! I've traveled with a hundred other men. None of them had the grit to make it through that. But George did!"

Serving Jesus takes sacrifice. George knew this. He gave up his own comfort to serve his Lord.

George Darley on snowshoes

GEORGE SHARES HIDDEN TREASURE WITH PROSPECTORS

"... the kingdom of heaven is like treasure hidden in a field, which a man found and hid; and for joy over it he goes and sells all that he has and buys that field." (Matthew 13:44)

During the Gold Rush, many **prospectors** came seeking gold. Their one goal was to strike it rich. They hoped to find so much gold that they would never have to work again.

Prospector
A person who searches for gold or other precious things.

George visited prospector camps often. There, he told the men about the unsearchable riches of Christ. Here is what he preached to them:

Friends, you are trying to strike it rich on earth. But I am here to tell you something. There is a greater treasure in heaven. All who prospect for this treasure will find it. When they find this heavenly treasure, they will receive great joy. All who find this heavenly treasure will have a mansion in heaven.

Sinner, do you want this heavenly treasure? Then go to Christ. Tell Him you have been seeking gold and silver that perishes. Tell Christ you desire riches that do not perish. Ask Him for the gold of His mercy, love, and goodness. Ask Him for the blood of Christ. Will you do this? Will you mine deep into God's love? Or will you be satisfied with earthly gold and silver? Will you reject the Savior? Would you reject the pearl of great price?

George was a bold evangelist. In July 1877, he took a trip with a miner. They were both on their way to Animas City.

George and the miner were unusual companions. They were two people

who were very different from each other. George was a pastor. The miner was not a Christian. He often used unclean language and took God's name in vain. The miner was not excited to travel with a preacher.

The trail was rough. The going was slow. But it was the path to Animas City.

The miner made a joke. "Pastor, this isn't the road to heaven!"

George replied, "No, it is not. But there are plenty of men like you on rough trails like this going to hell. I am doing what I can to save them."

The miner didn't crack any more jokes after that.

GEORGE'S LOVE FOR SOULS

Now then, we are ambassadors for Christ, as though God were pleading through us: we implore you on Christ's behalf, be reconciled to God. (2 Corinthians 5:20)

After church services on Sunday morning, George would walk to the miners' camp. He would then deliver a message to the miners. George did not want to miss this appointment. He knew it was important. But one day he had to decide how important it was. Was he truly committed to preach to these men?

One Sunday morning, George awoke to find eighteen inches of snow on the ground. It was still snowing. Some of his friends said, "George, I hope you aren't walking to the mine today. There are eighteen inches of snow on the ground. The wind is blowing too!"

George would not miss his opportunity to preach. He said, "I must not miss my appointment."

He ate a large meal. Then he changed into warmer clothes. He put on his boots and headed out the door.

For the next three hours, George trudged through the snow. Finally, he reached the mine. When he stepped through the door of the large hall at the mine, there was only one man there. He said to George, "We didn't expect you to come today!" George then visited the men in their cabins.

Leadville Colorado during the Gold Rush

The miners were amazed. This preacher of the gospel walked for three hours in deep snow. They said, "That preacher must really care. Otherwise, he would not have walked up here in such a storm."

ENDURANCE FOR CHRIST

Cold weather and long journeys were hard on George's health. But his love for Christ kept him going. He loved his Lord, and he loved sinners. That is why he kept scaling mountain peaks, fording dangerous rivers, and sleeping on the ground.

George knew this life was hard. Once he asked:

Among the highest ranges of the Rockies, there is good work to be done. Do you want your love for Christ to be tested? Press through a snowstorm above the tree line. Make your bed in the snow. Watch an avalanche sweep down the mountain. These make even the stoutest heart tremble. Your faith will be tested. The West needs strong men. Come and labor for Christ here.

May God make each of us strong for Jesus just like George Darley. May we serve Jesus with our whole heart as well!

Lake San Cristobal, Colorado

Amazon River Basin, Ecuador

25 ELISABETH ELLIOT: THE GOSPEL FOR THE AUCAS

Therefore I endure all things for the sake of the elect, that they also may obtain the salvation which is in Christ Jesus with eternal glory.
(2 Timothy 2:10)

Elisabeth Howard was thirteen years old when she read about John Stam and his wife. The Stams were a young couple who gave their lives for Christ in China in 1934. They died at the hands of Chinese Communists. Elisabeth Howard was astounded by their faith. She wanted to follow Christ like Mrs. Stam did.

Mrs. Stam wrote before she died:

Lord, I give up my own plans. I give up my own desires. I accept Your will for my life. I give my life completely to You. Fill me with your Holy Spirit. Use me as You will. Work out Your will in my life at any cost. Now and forever.

Elisabeth copied this prayer into the front of her Bible. It became her prayer too.

God blessed Elisabeth with a father and mother who loved the Lord. The Howard family often shared their home with visiting missionaries. While in school, Elisabeth also read about Amy Carmichael. Amy was a missionary to orphans in India. Elisabeth was inspired by this story too.

As Elisabeth grew older, she wanted to serve the Lord as a missionary.

To prepare for this, Elisabeth went to college. She studied Greek at Wheaton College. While there, she met a man named Jim Elliot. Both of them wanted to serve the Lord on the mission field. They both loved the Lord. They both wanted to give their lives to serve Him in far-off lands. One day, Jim and

Jim and Elisabeth Elliot

Elisabeth would marry. But first, they both began mission work.

SERVING THE LORD IN ECUADOR

In 1952, Jim and Elisabeth went to Ecuador. They served in different places. Jim served in the capital city, Quito. Elisabeth worked with a native tribe in the Ecuador jungles.

Elisabeth found this life difficult. She said, "It took so much time to do things just to stay alive." Elisabeth began to learn the language of the natives. This tribe spoke the Colorados language. It had never been written down. Elisabeth wanted to learn the language. Then she could help others translate the Bible.

Jim wrote Elisabeth a letter in 1953. He asked her to meet him in Quito. Elisabeth made it to Quito as fast as she could. She wondered what Jim wanted. When she got there, Jim asked, "Elisabeth, will you marry me?" Elisabeth rejoiced. She answered, "Yes!"

Jim and Elisabeth married on October 8, 1953. Now, Elisabeth Howard became Elisabeth Elliot.

They began their life together in Ecuador. They spent years serving the Quichua people. Living in the jungles was difficult. At times, it was lonely. Elisabeth wrote, "The missionary and his family are sometimes cut off from the rest of the world for months. It often took four to eight days through dangerous jungles to get help."

Travel became easier for Jim and Elisabeth when they met Nate Saint. Nate was an airplane pilot. He worked as a missionary pilot. He could fly missionaries into the field. He could also quickly bring food and other supplies.

Quito, Ecuador

Nate was a godly man and also a gifted pilot. He was very careful to fly safely. He would carefully weigh every person and item that went into the plane. He did this to make sure there was enough gas to get back and forth.

OPERATION AUCA

There were other tribes in Ecuador beside the Quichua. One tribe was very dangerous. It was called the Auca tribe. The Aucas avoided outsiders. They were violent. Nate Saint explained, "The Aucas were dangerous. Ecuador was embarrassed by them. No one knew how to reach them."

Five couples decided they would visit the Aucas. Jim and Elisabeth Elliot were one couple. Nate Saint and his wife Marjorie were another. The other three couples were Pete and Olive Fleming, Ed and Marilou McCully, and Roger and Barbara Youderian.

The Aucas were dangerous. The missionaries needed to be careful. They started by dropping gifts from the airplane. For several months, Nate and the others dropped gifts. They hoped the Aucas would learn to trust them. Perhaps then the Aucas would be peaceful to them?

River turtles in Ecuador

At last, the couples thought the time had come. The men would land and meet the Aucas. Elisabeth and the other wives were nervous and somewhat fearful. Would the Aucas attack? Elisabeth later wrote, "God gave us peace of heart. Each of us knew when we got married that God's work comes first."

On January 6, 1956, the five men landed near the Auca tribe. Three Aucas emerged from the jungle. The men greeted them. "Puinani!" they said. This word means "welcome" in Auca. The missionaries handed them gifts. The visit seemed to go well.

Over the next few days, the men landed in the same spot. Then, on January 8, they decided to go to the Auca camp. The men contacted their wives on the radio. "This is the day! We will contact you next at 4:30!"

At 4:30, no message came. All day, the women waited at the radio. The signal was silent. They began to pray more and more. They asked God to protect their husbands.

The next morning, another pilot went up to search. He saw Nate Saint's plane on the sandbar. The wings had been stripped. There was no sign of the missionaries.

A search party was formed. US and Ecuador soldiers combed the area for the men. The wives waited by the radio for news. The radio hummed to life.

Nate Saint in front of his plane

Nate Saint's plane

One of the men had been discovered. He had given his life for Christ. The Aucas had killed him. Then, one by one, the other four men were also found.

The wives were heartbroken. Their precious husbands were gone. They grieved. But they were not without hope. The five men were now with Jesus.

News about these deaths spread all over the world. Prayers were poured out by Christians everywhere. Christians prayed for the widows and their children. They also prayed for the Aucas. They asked God to save this violent tribe. The five widows did not want revenge. Instead, the women prayed for the Aucas to turn to the Lord.

The death of the five was not in vain. Soon, the Aucas would sing the praises of God!

LIVING WITH THE AUCAS

But I say to you, love your enemies, bless those who curse you, do good to those who hate you, and pray for those who spitefully use you and persecute you, that you may be sons of your Father in heaven; for He makes His sun rise on the evil and on the good, and sends rain on the just and on the unjust. (Matthew 5:44-45)

More missionaries came. They dropped more gifts to the Aucas. Little by little, this fierce tribe became more friendly to outsiders. Now, a way opened for Elisabeth to go and live near the Aucas. Would she?

Elisabeth might have hated the Aucas. They killed her husband. But instead, she showed love to them. It was Christ's power that gave Elisabeth this love.

Elisabeth moved near the Aucas. She learned their language. An Auca woman named Dayuma taught her. God began to work among this native tribe. By 1963, nine Aucas were baptized in the name of the Father, Son, and Holy Spirit. Soon, more Aucas would turn to Christ.

The tribe that once hated all outsiders now worshiped the one true God. They turned from idols to serve the living God. Elisabeth knew this happened by God's power. Only the God of miracles could do such a thing.

Oh, that men would give thanks to the LORD for His goodness,
And for His wonderful works to the children of men!
For He has broken the gates of bronze,
And cut the bars of iron in two. (Psalm 107:15-16)

Jaguar in the Amazon jungle

REPUBLIC OF ECUADOR	
Total population:	15 million
Total area:	109,000 square miles
Capital:	Quito
Official language:	Spanish
Primary religion:	Roman Catholic

PRAYER POINTS: ECUADOR

Now, take some time to pray for the people of Ecuador.

- **Pray for the Gospel to Spread among the Quichua**
  The Quichua people group are a large part of Ecuador's population. In 1967, there were only about 120 believers among these people. Now, there may be as many as one million Quichua believers. Praise God for these believers in Christ!
- **Pray for the Poor People in the Cities**
  Many people live in poverty in the large cities of Ecuador. These people need the hope of Christ. Pray for more of Christ's servants to minister to the poor.
- **Pray for the Jungle Tribes**
  There are still tribes living in the jungles of Ecuador. Pray for God to raise up men and women to take the Bible to these tribes.

Andes Mountains, Peru

26 BETTY GREENE: FLYING FOR THE GLORY OF GOD

God's gifts of grace come in many forms. Each of you has received a gift in order to serve others. You should use it faithfully. (1 Peter 4:10 NIRV)

Charles Lindbergh (1902-1974)

Betty stared into the blue sky. Overhead, the famous American pilot Charles Lindbergh flew by. It was 1927. Lindbergh had just flown from New York to Paris. He was the first pilot to fly across the Atlantic Ocean nonstop. A new era for flight had begun.

Betty's twin brother Bill explained, "Did you know, Betty, that Lindbergh's flight took 33 ½ hours? He flew 3,600 miles!"

Lindbergh's plane, *Spirit of St. Louis*, dazzled the crowd below. Betty was mesmerized. She wanted to fly as well. She was only seven years old. She imagined the day when she could fly too.

In 1936, Betty and Bill's sixteenth birthday was about to arrive. Betty's father asked the twins, "What would you like for your birthday?"

That was an easy question to answer. Bill and Betty agreed. They asked their father for flying lessons. They found the lessons thrilling. But Betty didn't have enough money to get her pilot's license. After her lessons were over, she stopped flying. Maybe someday she would fly again.

FLYING DURING WORLD WAR II

In 1937, Betty went to college. Her parents encouraged her to study nursing. Betty found nursing studies difficult. She didn't want to learn medicine. Her heart was still set on flying.

Attack on Pearl Harbor, December 1941

Betty's parents told her, "Why don't you write down the things that interest you?"

Betty did so. First, she wrote down, "I am a Christian. I want to serve the Lord Jesus." Next she wrote, "I love flying." Then she wrote, "I love working in the church and any kind of mission work." She noted, "I like people, but I don't want to work in the hospital."

Betty wondered, "Can I serve Jesus and fly?" She did not know how. But God would soon open the door.

In 1941, the United States entered World War II. Japan bombed Pearl Harbor, Hawaii. America fought back. The military needed women pilots. Women did not fly in combat. They didn't fight in the battles. But they could test planes. They could also fly planes back and forth to different places.

A new group was started for women pilots. It was called the Women Air-force Service Pilots. People called it WASP for short. Betty applied.

Betty was accepted. She began pilot's training. Soon, she was one of the most gifted pilots in the service. She did many different jobs for WASP.

She flew airplanes that would be tracked on radar. This taught military men how to use radar. Betty also flew over the base at night. Men on the ground used their searchlights to spot the aircraft.

Later, WASP moved Betty to Wright Field in Ohio. Her job was to fly giant B-17 bombers as high as possible. The military wanted to learn how high they could safely fly. Betty and her friends would stretch the limits.

Betty knew that flying could be risky. That is why she began every flight in prayer. She told her friend, "I've always prayed before taking off in an aircraft." Betty trusted God to keep her safe in the air.

Betty Greene

B-17 in flight

Betty flew the massive B-17 up to 40,000 feet. During World War II, she continued to become even more skillful as a pilot.

MISSION AVIATION FELLOWSHIP

Betty loved her job with WASP. Yet she still wondered, "Can I use flying for mission work?" She prayed for wisdom.

In 1944, Betty received a letter from a man named Jim Truxton. He explained, "There are several other airmen who share your vision. Pilots want to spread the gospel to the ends of the earth."

Betty met Jim in Washington DC. Jim explained the vision of the Christian Airmen's Missionary Fellowship. This group was called CAMF for short. Later it would be renamed the Mission Aviation Fellowship (MAF). The CAMF was small. They did not yet own a single aircraft. Yet they had a big vision.

Betty signed on to help. Soon, CAMF got their first opportunity. Bible translators in Mexico needed a flight to the jungles of Peru. There was no easy way to get there. Wycliffe Bible Translators asked CAMF for help.

Soon Betty was flying. She took the Bible translators deep into the jungle.

Grumman Duck

Peruvian village on Amazon River

The trip could take days or weeks on foot. Now by airplane, the trip took just a few hours.

In December 1946, Betty took Bible translators over the Andes Mountains. Flying over the Andes was treacherous. She flew a Grumman Duck. This airplane is an amphibious aircraft. This means it can land on water.

Before takeoff, as always, Betty prayed. She knew to trust God always for protection. Yet she also made sure things were done safely.

It was morning, December 19, 1946. Betty and two Bible translators took off from Lima, Peru. Slowly, Betty brought the plane to 10,000 feet. Reaching 16,000 feet, the Grumman Duck passed over the towering Andes Mountains. It was a beautiful and awe-inspiring sight to behold. Betty was the first woman to fly over the High Andes. Over the next month, she made twenty-three trips in the Grumman Duck.

For the next few years, Betty made her home in Peru. Her skillful piloting was a gift to the other missionaries. Her example teaches us that everyone's gifts are important. The body of Christ is built up by everyone using their gift. Betty's gift was flying. The Bible translators' gifts were language and teaching. Together, they were a team. Together, they reached the tribes of Peru for Christ.

Someone once asked, "Betty, would you like to be a missionary someday too?" Betty answered, "I am a missionary. My job is to fly."

Betty was right. You don't have to be a Bible translator or teacher to help with Christ's kingdom work. Whatever gift God gave you, you can use it for His glory.

LATER YEARS

After serving in Ecuador, Betty flew in other parts of the world for MAF. In 1951, she moved to Africa. There she flew in Nigeria and Sudan. Then, in 1960, she embarked on her last tour of service. She flew missionaries in Indonesia for two years.

MAF continues its important work today. In 2010, MAF flew into fifty-five countries. By then, they had 130 airplanes. Thanks be to God for technology like airplanes. Now, God's servants can travel the world faster than ever.

BASIC FACTS ABOUT PERU

REPUBLIC OF PERU	
Total population:	33 million
Total area:	496,000 square miles
Capital:	Lima
Official language:	Spanish
Primary religion:	Roman Catholic

PRAYER POINTS: PERU

Now, take some time to pray for the people of Peru.

- **Thank God for Bible Translation**
  Bible translators have done much to spread the faith in Peru. Because of these faithful men and women, more native groups in Peru know the Lord Jesus. Give thanks to God for this! Ask Him to give His Word to many more.

- **Pray for the Drug Trade to End**
  Many people in Peru and other countries buy and sell drugs. This hurts the people of Peru. Many people kill, steal, and lie to get more drugs. Pray for God to stop evildoers. Pray that people would not be addicted to drugs. Instead, pray that they would love the Lord.

- **Pray for Roman Catholics to Know the Gospel**
  Most people in Peru say they believe in Jesus as Roman Catholics. But only five percent attend any kind of church. Most do not know the true gospel. Pray that God would send more faithful preachers and teachers to Peru.

Tapir

LIST OF IMAGES

3. Modern replica of the *Mayflower* | Wikimedia Commons | Public Domain
4. William Bradford | Wikimedia Commons | Public Domain
5. Illustration of Plymouth Plantation | Illustration by Zakir Hussain
6. Miles Standish | Wikimedia Commons | Public Domain
7. The first thanksgiving at Plymouth | Wikimedia Commons | Public Domain
8. Marsh near Plymouth, Massachusetts | iStock.com
9. Canadian Goose | iStock.com

CHAPTER 8

1. Martha's Vineyard, Massachusetts | iStock.com
2. John Eliot | iStock.com
3. John Eliot's home | Wikimedia Commons | Public Domain
4. Map of New England | iStock.com
5. John Eliot preaching | Illustration by Zakir Hussain
6. Deer in New England | iStock.com
7. Modern-day Natick | Wikimedia Commons | Public Domain
8. Title page of John Eliot's Bible translation | Wikimedia Commons | Public Domain
9. Connecticut River in Massachusetts | iStock.com

CHAPTER 9

1. Old City of Philadelphia, Pennsylvania | iStock.com
2. George Whitefield | Wikimedia Commons | Public Domain
3. Benjamin Franklin | Wikimedia Commons | Public Domain
4. George Whitefield preaching | Illustration by Zakir Hussain
5. Jonathan Edwards | Wikimedia Commons | Public Domain
6. John Wesley | Wikimedia Commons | Public Domain
7. Christ Church in Philadelphia | Wikimedia Commons | Public Domain

CHAPTER 10

1. Housatonic River, Connecticut | iStock.com
2. Yale College | Wikimedia Commons | Public Domain
3. David Brainerd ministering to indians | Illustration by Zakir Hussain
4. Example of Native American Wigwam | iStock.com
5. Lapowinsa, chief of the Delaware Indians | Wikimedia Commons | Public Domain
6. Stokes State Forest, New Jersey | iStock.com
7. Appalachian Trail | iStock.com

CHAPTER 11

1. Squantz Pond, Connecticut | iStock.com
2. Yale College, New Haven | iStock.com
3. Jonathan Edwards | iStock.com
4. Illustration of Northampton | Wikimedia Commons | Public Domain
5. Edwards in Stockbridge, Massachusetts | Illustration by Zakir Hussain
6. Modern-day Stockbridge | iStock.com

CHAPTER 12

1. Oneida Lake, New York | iStock.com
2. Samuel Kirkland | Wikimedia Commons | Public Domain
3. Seneca Chief | Wikimedia Commons | Public Domain
4. Samuel Kirkland among the Oneida | Illustration by Zakir Hussain
5. George Washington | Wikimedia Commons | Public Domain
6. Surrender of the British at Yorktown, 1781 | Wikimedia Commons | Public Domain
7. Oneida Lake at sunrise | iStock.com
8. Duck on lake | iStock.com

CHAPTER 13

1. Pinware River, Labrador, Canada | iStock.com
2. Modern-day Herrnhut | Wikimedia Commons | Public Domain
3. Nikolaus Zinzendorf | iStock.com
4. Eskimo family | Wikimedia Commons | Public Domain
5. Map of Canada | iStock.com
6. Eskimos of Labrador | Illustration by Zakir Hussain
7. Moravian church in Labrador | Wikimedia Commons | Public Domain
8. Canadian Moose | iStock.com

CHAPTER 14

1. Pinware River, Labrador, Canada | iStock.com
2. Modern-day Herrnhut | Wikimedia Commons | Public Domain
3. Nikolaus Zinzendorf | iStock.com
4. Eskimo family | Wikimedia Commons | Public Domain
5. Map of Canada | iStock.com
6. Eskimos of Labrador | Illustration by Zakir Hussain
7. Moravian church in Labrador | Wikimedia Commons | Public Domain
8. Canadian Moose | iStock.com

CHAPTER 15

1. New England landscape | iStock.com
2. Congregational church in Killingworth, Connecticut | Wikimedia Commons | Public Domain
3. Map of Connecticut | iStock.com
4. Illustration of Asahel Nettleton | Illustration by Zakir Hussain
5. Village hymns | Wikimedia Commons | Public Domain
6. Elizabeth Park, Hartford, Connecticut | iStock.com
7. Hartford, Connecticut | Wikimedia Commons | Public Domain

LIST OF IMAGES

LIST OF IMAGES

CHAPTER 24

1. Mt. Sneffels, San Juan Mountains, Colorado | iStock.com
2. George Darley | Wikimedia Commons | Public Domain
3. Old mining equipment near Silverton, Colorado | iStock.com
4. Lake City Presbyterian Church, Lake City, Colorado | Google Maps
5. George Darley on snowshoes | Illustration by Zakir Hussain
6. Map of Colorado | iStock.com
7. Leadville, Colorado during the Gold Rush | iStock.com
8. Lake San Cristobal, Colorado | iStock.com

CHAPTER 25

1. Amazon River Basin, Ecuador | iStock.com
2. Jim and Elisabeth Elliot | Wikimedia Commons | Public Domain
3. Quito, Ecuador | iStock.com
4. River turtles in Ecuador | iStock.com
5. Nate Saint in front of his plane | Wikimedia Commons | Public Domain
6. Nate Saint's plane | Illustration by Zakir Hussain
7. Map of Ecuador | iStock.com
8. Jaguar in the Amazon jungle | iStock.com

CHAPTER 26

1. Andes Mountains, Peru | iStock.com
2. Charles Lindbergh | Wikimedia Commons | Public Domain
3. Attack on Pearl Harbor, December 1941 | Wikimedia Commons | Public Domain
4. Betty Greene | Wikimedia Commons | Public Domain
5. B-17 in flight | Wikimedia Commons | Public Domain
6. Grumman Duck | Illustration by Zakir Hussain
7. Peruvian village on the Amazon River | iStock.com
8. Tapir | iStock.com